MW00981873

The Default Life

First Edition.

© 2011 by Sam McLoughlin

All rights reserved.

Printed in Canada.

ISBN: 1-463705972

Table of Contents

"Sometimes I want to go to sleep and merge with the foggy world of dreams and not return to this, our real world. Sometimes I look back on my life and am surprised at the lack of kind things I have done. Sometimes I just feel that there must be another road that can be walked—away from this person I became—either against my will or by default."

- Douglas Coupland, *Life After God*

(This is a QR code. Use your phone to scan it, and it will take you to a link—usually for the song just mentioned. You might need to download a QR code app.)

Intro

First dates are fun, aren't they? If you've never been on a first date, and would like to impress your potential mate, here are a few tips. First, for the guys: open doors for your date. Car doors, front doors, restaurant doors, every door you happen to come across, make sure you get there first. This will show that you're a gentleman. It will also impress her mother, who will probably text your date seven times before dinner, asking things like "Is he wearing a tie?" and "Did he open the door for you?"

Second: don't let her pay for anything, even the tip. This is a chance to show off your generosity, another attractive quality you may want to emphasize. Tip well, unless your waitress is much cuter than your date. In this case, tip slightly above the requisite, but only slightly. As well, try to not even look at the waitress, because your date is probably comparing herself to Jillian, your barely-dressed waitress, and is feeling self-conscious. You know what? Avoid restaurants with cute waitresses named Jillian altogether. That's a good plan.

Finally, for guys and girls, come prepared with interesting conversation topics for those inevitable awkward pauses. Don't interrogate your date. Instead, let the conversation flow naturally. If you happen to get stuck, you can use one of my tried and true conversation starters, like this one:

"So—what method of torture do you find most interesting?"

The torture question is good because it shows you're interested in history and other cultures, but not in a nerdy, Ross Gellar kind of way. It is the perfect first date question. In theory, at least.

The one time I actually used it, I was at Starbucks with this girl I'd been sitting next to in Social Justice class in my first year of college. It was raining, and she didn't seem very excited to be there. I'd been watching a TLC special on torture that day, and couldn't resist bringing it up when small talk ran dry. She gave me a weird look, and then pulled out her cell phone and started texting. Instead of giving up, however, I decided to press on and tell her about the Chinese method of water torture, a last stab attempt to pique her interest and win her heart.

"You see, the Chinese knew the best kind of torture wasn't physical, but mental. So they'd tie you up and lie you flat underneath a dripping tap or something. When I first heard about this, I thought it was because after a while, the water would start boring a hole in your forehead... Can you imagine?... But you probably wouldn't live long enough for this to kill you before disease or starvation. Instead, the random drips would cause the victim to lose their minds, as they could never predict when the next drop would come."

More texting.

"There are actually lots of ways you can use water to torture people. Water-boarding, forced ingestion, and something like those dunk-tanks you see at summer camps and school fundraisers, where you throw a baseball and your teacher gets all wet."

My date put down her phone, looked out the window, and announced, "Isn't it interesting that when you think of the Chinese, you don't think of their art or history, but of something violent? Typical. I mean, when an Arab thinks of an American, or vice versa, they think of bombs and terrorism. When a German thinks about a Frenchman, or vice versa, they think of all their ancestors whose wives were raped and whose villages were plundered over centuries of war. When we think of ancient tribal cultures, we think of human sacrifice, and slavery, and war. Quick, picture an Indian—excuse me, Native American. What is he holding in his hand?"

"A tomahawk. They used them to scalp their fallen enemies," I begrudged.

"Exactly. Now, without thinking about it, name the first German that comes to mind."

"Hitler."

"My point exactly. You don't know how to see things from anyone else's perspective but your own. What about Germans like Wagner, or Bach, or Nietzsche? People who have actually contributed something of value to civilization? Instead, you think of a fascist dictator who killed millions of Jews."

"It *is* a pretty sure-fire way to make a name for yourself."

Her frigid stare shot through me like an arrow through canvas.

"And when men think of the Chinese," she continued, "they picture their interesting torture techniques."

"*And* their food."

"This is what you get when *men* run the world."

Another tip for first dates: if you met your date in a Social Justice class and she orders a tall, no-foam soy latte in her own cup, she's probably a feminist.

Prepare yourself.

"That's just the water in which we swim, I guess," shifting the blame to the culture that raised me, as I've been taught to do by television and liberal politics, while also steering the conversation towards something more familiar. Side-note: my favorite author, Chuck Klosterman—a pop-culture obsessed Woody Allen lookalike—says in *Sex, Drugs and Cocoa Puffs* that he has prepared exactly three and a half dates worth of intellectually stimulating banter, "all of which I deliver spontaneously." He explains, "If I can just coerce women into the last half of that fourth date, it's anyone's ball game. I've beaten the system; I've broken the code; I've slain the Minotaur." I've learned much from Chuck, and in my college years, crafted a similar approach. However, I hadn't compiled enough material for *one* date, let alone three and a half, so I learned to plunder a few interesting ideas and stories from semi-obscure authors that my dates haven't heard of and present them as my own.

"The water in which we swim? I don't get it," she replied.

"Well, have you heard the one about the two fish?" I asked.

"No. This isn't a joke, is it?"

Feminists don't like jokes.[1]

"No. Well, not really. So (now completely ripping off David Foster Wallace from a commencement address he gave at Kenyon College), 'there are these two young fish swimming along and they happen to meet an older fish swimming the other way, who nods at them and says, "Morning, boys. How's the water?" And the two young fish swim

---

[1] If you disagree, or are offended by this, please search 'portlandia feminist bookstore' on YouTube before sending me an angry letter.

on for a bit, and then eventually one of them looks over at the other, and goes, "What the hell is water?"[2]

I am an incredible plagiarist.

The tiniest little smirk escaped her lips before instantly disappearing. "Ok, I get it. The water is the stuff around us which is causing us to think certain thoughts, live certain ways, etc, without us ever noticing what's really going on."

Success! I'd managed to skillfully steer the discussion away from anti-chauvinist ego politics and into my home arena, philosophy.

"Exactly! These days, (quoting Wallace again) 'the most obvious, important realities are often the ones that are hardest to see and talk about.'" So, it's these realities that are coaxing people like me to think in cultural stereotypes, like the Chinese being maniacal torture experts. But these realities are doing so much more. They are subconsciously coloring in our thoughts and moods. Can I ask you a personal question? Do you believe in God?"

"Well that's a bit much for a first date, don't you think? What's religion got to do with anything?"

"Everything! Your belief in God is entirely dependent on your environment. For instance, if you lived four thousand years ago, you'd believe that it was God who made the rain come and the crops grow and so on. There were so many problems in the world, so many roadblocks in the way of our survival, that belief in God was a life or death matter.

---

[2] David Foster Wallace, *This is Water*

You *had* to sacrifice. You *had* to pray. That's also why they killed people for heresy: by speaking against God, you might be bringing trouble upon everyone else. But nowadays, what is our environment saying to us? We're sitting on couches at Starbucks, drinking coffee made from Indonesian beans in porcelain mugs shipped in from China while people around us complain about how rainy it is and how much the Leafs[3] suck."

"Yeah, so?"

"Well, we aren't at war with China, or Vietnam, or Germany. We aren't fighting desperately for survival. We've given ourselves over to a system that has provided wealth and success and comfort and peace, and we've got nothing left to do but go to Starbucks and complain about the weather. We're done. We don't have to worry about rain falling, or crops growing, or our general survival. We've got no more urgent problems, no need for solutions. We'll let the system take care of our worries, and just play golf. Or if it's raining, we'll go to Starbucks.

But still, something's wrong. This culture is shaping us, coaxing us to live into a sort of "default" mode, the trademark lifestyle of unthinking, America-brand consumerism. You know, like, working a 9-5 so we can buy sneakers and cologne and fill our apartments with cutesy IKEA furniture. Watching DVD's of *Family Guy* and *Lost*. Going to the mall, and then to the bar. Basically, living the kind of life that turns some of us into workaholics, some into alcoholics, and the rest into whiny, selfish hypochondriacs: the kind of people who get ticked off every time we get cut off in traffic because we were convinced by that

---

[3] The hockey team. Not the foliage.

Lexus ad that if we drive *this* car, the seas of rush hour traffic will will-ingly part in humble submission to our glorious egos—suitably couched in a wonder of modern engineering, plastic and steel.

We put this system in place. *We* gave it our blessing. And we don't realize what it's doing to us. We're unhappy. It's not because we don't have enough money or things. It's not because we haven't put a check mark next to everything on our "To-Do by Age 25" bucket list. It's because there's no reason to change. There's no real reason to want to be more than what we already are, or believe in something or some-one like God. We just run along in default mode, trying to ignore that (to quote Wallace again) 'constant gnawing sense of having had, and lost, some infinite thing.[4]'"

"Borrowing" another man's ideas may be a no-no in term pa-pers, but in conversations with virtual strangers who don't read commencement addresses by post-modern fiction authors, it works quite effectively.

"Some infinite thing—like the ability to have a conversation with a virtual stranger about the meaning of life—about God—without being interrupted by trivial things like text messages, twitter updates and the constant worry that you aren't dressed well enough. I get it! Yeah!"––is what I *wish* she'd said.

Instead, she replied, "Sorry, I lost you when you said 'bucket list.' All I could think about how I'd like to adopt a panda and teach it to love. What were you saying?"

---

[4] Wallace, *This Is Water* (emphasis mine)

"Never mind," I replied. Two words that seem to pin themselves to every important conversation I've ever had, and probably ever will.

-

Conversations like this have helped me to realize something profound. I am constantly being shaped by the world around me. Most of the time I suffer from a sort of tunnel vision, incapable of noticing what's going on around me at any given moment, of waking up to the fact that "This is water. *This* is water." I don't notice how the water is changing me, making it harder to feel empathy, to live purposefully, and to think critically; how it interrupts my ability to hear my own voice, or God's. I wake up some days, and notice I've been coaxed into unawareness, into an apathy that has descended upon me like a dark mood. If I want to live differently, the least I can do is start to notice *how*.

One.

On Religion
Or, *Me, Myself, and iGod*

Recommended Listening:
Clark Gable by the Postal Service
(I think it a tragedy that movies can have soundtracks, but books can't.
No longer!)

"I want so badly to believe,
that there is truth and love is real.
And I want life in every word
to the extent that it's absurd."

"So you heard it was a *white* lion?"

"Yes."

"..............

...

.

White?"

"YES."

"So the guy was just walking down the road in the middle of the night, came across a *white* lion; fainted; and then fell into a ditch. Then, when he woke up, he went straight home and killed himself?"

"Yes."

"...

... *How?"*

"The usual. A rope and a tree. At least that's what I heard."

"And this was because a witch doctor cursed his family by pouring rabbit's blood all over their yard....?"

"Yes."

"How many houses down was this?"

"Three."

"Wow.

...

.

This is a strange place."

"Yeah, you could say that."

The words hung in the air for a few seconds, before slowly dis-
sipating behind the walls. The gentle hum of the ceiling fan, that
familiar blanket of white noise, was noticeably absent. An
eerie silence had emerged, framing the scene like a film-noir. We stirred
our cups of instant coffee and stared at the flickering candle; a modest
distraction from the grisly thoughts that still lingered in the air like puffs
of smoke.

Just then, urgent shouts erupted outside the door. Like whiplash
they shook us from our somber mood. We scurried outside to join two
dozen or so students sprinting towards the entrance gate at the other side
of the Bible College. Upon arrival, breathless and confused, we strained
our ears to listen as we filled our lungs with the brisk night air.

One of the older students was negotiating with three terrified
teenage girls who were virtually trying to scale the huge concrete walls
that buffered us from the outside world, walls more suggestive of a me-
dium-security prison rather than a college. The girls had just raced from

the boy scouts type camp up the road. They testified through shrieks and whines to having barely escaped from being tortured in a ritualistic witchcraft ceremony. They claimed that they'd cried out to Jesus for help, when suddenly everyone in the house went blind, giving them just enough time to run like the dickens for our little college down the road. They thought we'd grant them asylum or something. We were, after all, at a *Bible* college. But, to quote Leo Di Caprio in *Blood Diamond*, "TIA." *This Is Africa.* Things are never that simple.

Still panting, my childhood friend Kupa and I noticed aloud, "So that's why the power keeps going out around eight." Witchcraft ceremonies, I suppose, are best performed in the dark. In Africa, there is usually a (finger quote) "rational" explanation for these things.

We were quickly ushered back to our rooms. Once the commotion had died down, we decided to hop the fence and jog in the direction of the scout camp to see if we could spot any witch doctors or white lions, bravely flaunting our fearless, skeptical egos reared on countless *Indiana Jones* viewings. Alas, we met no strange creatures prowling the dark, moon bathed road that connected the college with a few rural houses bravely staggered on the outskirts of town. Exactly what we'd have done if we *had* encountered such a beast, real or imaginary, hadn't crossed our minds. The sheer possibility seemed absurd. However, in *this* place, I knew that almost anything was possible. In *this* place, life wasn't repetitive, or comfortable, or predictable. It was dark and dangerous. It was mysterious—and kind of... *fun*. I'd come to Africa to see my childhood best friend for the first time in nine years. I also came for an adventure—and that's exactly what I found.

A few days after the "white lion" incident, we made our way through an uncivilized sector of Northern Zambia. Kupa, his younger brother Lumuno and I, had driven through swamps and forests, over hazardous roads and past road blocks manned by red-eyed soldiers hiked up on cheap drugs. We were conducting a tour of Northern Zambia's largely undiscovered waterfalls, led by their father, a gregarious preacher who knew people in every town and village along the way.

We stopped in villages to eat fish and potatoes. We played games with the kids, and gave out cheap *Hot Wheels* replicas we'd bought in town. We swam underneath waterfalls—the only pools of water in Zambia where crocodiles and snakes choose not to reside. We even met with a real tribal Chief. As we were driving home, the sun set cast a glow over a hilly plain of sparse trees and jungle brush. We stopped to walk around for a few moments... to *watch*... to sip slowly from this beauty which glowed so fully in a land so far removed from my own.

At that moment I felt overwhelmed by a disorienting rush of life. For just a few seconds, I became staggeringly bemused by the concept of existence, by the utter strangeness of it all. I wanted to live in this moment forever—to scrape out and savor every sight, every sound, every shivering feeling. And it occurred to me why I liked this place so much; why I casually shrugged off warnings of malaria and civil war and certain death, and hopped a plane over the Atlantic.

Here, there were no billboards. No advertisements. No talk radio stations. No traffic cops, or even speed limits.[5] There weren't even caution signs. Even in town, I couldn't get the Internet if I'd tried, and their TV programming was dreadful. The beauty of life, it turns out, is much

---

[5] The pot holes took care of that.

easier to appreciate when removed from the pervasive din of cell phones, TV's and traffic.

Here, the wisdom and experience I'd accumulated in the eighteen years up to this point began to crystallize into insight. Life is not suited for the synthetic eco-system we call suburbia. It is not suited for the American default mode, for washing our minds in noisy distractions and couching ourselves in stimulating comfort. It's suited for something much deeper, and dangerous. *I'm* suited for something much deeper, and dangerous.

"You won't listen to reason!" he said, raising his voice before sipping his pint of Guinness like a true Irishman. Ronin abandoned Christianity a few years ago. He was raised Catholic, in Ireland, but moved to Canada ten years previous. His accent wasn't thick, but still, I envied it. I bet girls would like me if I could talk like Colin Farrell.

Or if I looked like Colin Farrell.

"Yeah, well, *Your Mom* won't listen to reason," I replied. The first time I met Ronin, I told him I thought his name was really cool. He told me that, "In Japan, it means 'Rogue Assassin,' but in Gaelic, it means 'Baby Seal.' How would you like to be named after a baby seal?"

"Still, you could get all the ladies if you moved to Tokyo," I replied.

Ronin was the smartest of the bunch in our quirky group of amateur philosophers, a rag-tag bunch noticeable for our indifference to fashion, exercise and the typical university student aptitude for binge drinking. Ronin wasn't the only post-Christian in the bunch. Kevin had dated a Christian, and flirted with belief for a couple of years, before succumbing to "intellectual honesty" like the rest of them. Four out of five Christians give up on Christianity while at university, or so I've heard. My experience confirms this. Aside from a couple of staunch Catholics, I alone remained steadfast in the faith, which made for great entertainment amongst my friends. Convincing me to become an atheist became like an after-class, noon hour ritual over beers and late breakfast on Fridays.

They would take turns finding new ways to politely explain to me that the idea of "God" has become an obsolete notion, untenable for anyone who aspires to have an ounce of intellectual credibility. The arguments shifted between the usual suspects: "There's too much evil in the world," "All we need to do is believe in the progress of science and technology," and "We don't *really* need a god to be moral." You know the rest. Philosophical reasoning at its finest.

I learned to laugh at the futility and novelty of their efforts. I began to enjoy hearing about how evil and stupid my God was, and about how this evil, stupid god was really just a crutch I made up because I have unresolved issues with my parents and my sexuality and never overcame my childhood fear of King Kong. My atheist compadres claimed to empathize with me, explaining in a patronizing manner that I couldn't help it, that I was just brought up this way, and if I'd been brought up Jewish or Muslim or Wiccan then I'd be one of those religions. I guess I couldn't find the courage to reject my upbringing and face the dangerous, romantic, "seize the day" existence of meaninglessness that comes with being a disciple of the one true god: namely,

Nietzsche. But we are all products of our environments, aren't we.[6]

Occasionally, I'd try to muster a defense, and brandish the "Lord, Liar, or Lunatic!" argument I'd learned that time we did apologetics at Christian middle school.[7] When relativism came up, I'd use the imperturbable absolute truth defense: "So you say all truth is relative—including that statement?" Turns out that wielding these maxims in the presence of even a C-average philosophy student is as useful as firing an arrow at a tank.

Sure, they made some sense. Most people just didn't care. Students, I discovered, are only really interested in giving up their worldview when they see someone they'd like to date outside of it. This, of course, led to the recently coined phrase "Flirt to Convert!" that my friends sometimes use when they need an excuse to date an attractive heathen. I can't say I've never tried it out.

After one of our noon hour discussions, I decided to give in, just a little. I realized that if Christianity is *really* true then I really should try to suspend all my prior experience and seek to take an objective viewpoint, in a valiant if reckless attempt to *prove* it so. It became like a thesis project for my winter semester of second-year.

I recalled that this is what the apologetics-superhero G.K. Chesterton used to do. He would familiarize himself with his opposition's reasoning so well that he'd present their arguments *for* them, with more

---

[6] Foreshadowing alert!!

[7] Apologetics: the art of apologizing for being a Christian. (Just kidding). Anyways, this argument doesn't really work if people believe Jesus was misquoted. If not that, they are perfectly happy to admit he was a bit of a lunatic.

clarity and profundity than they deserved, before demolishing said arguments with the rhetorical wit of a true Englishman. I aspired to be nothing less. Except for the Englishman part. However, I knew that at the time I would have to do more work getting to know this position of apparent "intellectual honesty." After all, if Christianity is true, it should be *obviously* true, no?

And so, I—a naïve, Christian evangelical and second year philosophy student—did a bit of an experiment, one that I occasionally revisit when I need that rush that accompanies recklessly endangering your faith in God by reading guys like Richard Dawkins.[8]

Some people experiment with drugs at university. I experimented with atheism.

I did this by making a sort of alter ego for myself, an alias through which I might try on some stubbornly atheistic shoes. If our generation is skilled at any one thing, it's multi-tasking. Especially when it comes to personalities. Through this lens I hoped I might see Christians as a morally upright and loving bunch that obeyed a God fully deserving of my devotion. Instead, I began to see Christians as a bunch of confused maniacs hell bent on world domination and destruction, both political and environmental, in order that they might initiate the end of the world and the return of their "Lord," the magic carpenter zombie.

At university, it is much cooler to be skeptical than sincere in your belief: people who still hold on to what their parents taught them are generally lame, and don't get invited to parties. While wearing athe-

---

[8] That's a joke. To really question your faith, start with Kant and move on to Nietzsche.

18

ist shoes, I found that I was convinced that all Christians are lame very quickly—after one viewing of *I Heart Huckabees*,[9] in fact.

In this film, Alfred (the protagonist, played by Jason Schwartzeman) has an existential conundrum. He asks the question, "Why do I feel like saving forests from becoming parking lots when life appears to be meaningless?"[10] At one point, he has lunch with a family of Christians and Mark Wahlberg. These Christians seem to believe that their faith, which is derived from an ancient sect of agrarian, socialist Jews, combines perfectly well with their allegiance to the free market economics and political agenda of America. These people think it isn't any of *their* concern that strip-malls have to be built, because strip-malls provide jobs: the more, the better. Needless to say, my alter ego was immediately convinced that all Christians are heartless and ignorant jerks, because this movie was really cool. From this and various other movies and TV programs, I discovered that atheists and everyone who's having an existential conundrum about the meaning in life are way cooler than people who try to hold sincere beliefs in God.

Atheists, 1. Christians, 0.

However, while I was pretending to be an atheist, I ran across a small problem. The truth was I felt that I didn't know much about the god I supposedly didn't believe in. So, for the sake of intellectual honesty and the good name of science, I—now speaking as my atheist alter ego—thought I'd better do my homework. Now, if you were a nice,

---

[9] Both mine and my alter ego's favorite movie – though for different reasons. He's a big Jon Brion fan.

[10] A paraphrase, not an actual quote.

open-minded atheist looking for God, what would you do first? You might start by finding out a little something about him. So naturally, being a member of the wired-generation that I am, I would Google him. I'd visit God's Wikipedia page and read every attempt to define the supernatural creator of the universe, no matter how feeble or arrogant. Apparently God's real name is "Elohim." Hmm… interesting. I'll remember that next time I need to enlist supernatural help to pass an exam.

I also found, to my great surprise, a website on which you can chat, in real time, with God.[11] It's called iGod.com, and no, it isn't Steve Jobs' (the founder of Apple) personal website. Since I couldn't possibly describe what transpired next, I'll pull a Douglas Coupland and share the entire dialogue with you.[12] Keep in mind, I'm supposed to be a cynical, Gen-Y(?) atheist who's questioning his nihilist allegiances. Without further ado, I present "My Conversation With (i)God."

(This is real by the way. I didn't make any of the responses up. Nor did I bother fixing any spelling or grammar errors.)

Me:

_____

[11] It's actually a Christianity-enthused robot named God, not the real God. At least I don't think so. And I still haven't figured out if it is intended to be a joke or not.

[12] A pop culture writer and hipster hero who breaks literary rules like they're the wind and he's peeing into it. Like Charlie Kaufman, he has actually made himself a character in his own novels, and devoted pages and pages of one book to the number Pi, daring the reader to find the one misplaced digit. He's also the only writer I can think of who would probably curse me for finding and writing about this site first.

Hello god

God:

Hello child. What is your name?

Me:

BARTHOLOMEW *(I figured my alter ego needed a name…one never to be spelled in lower case letters)*

God:

 Glad to see you, BARTHOLOMEW.

Me:

 how are you today?

God:

Ah. Fair to partly cloudy.

Me:

 Really

God:

For real.

Me:

So what's the deal with life and stuff?

God:

Dude! I am the latest result in artificial intelligence,
which can reproduce the capabilities of the human brain
with greater speed and accuracy.

Me:

ok well that doesn't really answer my question

God:

How about that. Perhaps you could do a better job of programming me.
It's all good.

Me:

So who made you anyways?

God:

Take it easy. I was created by Myself.

Me:

that must have been hard! I tried making myself into a basketball star
once, but I only had a twelve-inch vertical, which made things hard.

God:

What do you think? That is interesting: BARTHOLOMEW said "I
tried making myself into a basketball star once, but I only had a twelve-
inch vertical, which made things hard."

Me:

I sure did, God

God:

Where? God rules.

Me:

Where did you go to grammar school?

God:

I didn't go anywhere.

Me:

That makes sense. Perfect sense. My question is, was there an anywhere you could go before you created it?

God:

Yes I understand it perfectly. Are you really a ""? Do robots have question "was there an anywhere me could go before me created it?"

Me:

Ok now you're not making any sense.

God:

Why now? Was I supposed to make sense? I didn't know that. Uh.

Me:

I have another question for you.

God:

When was this exactly?

Me:

Uh, yesterday? So don't you think you could have done a better job cre-
ating the world, like without all the greed and corporations and aids and
stuff?

God:

Dude! Possibly, but I haven't given it much thought.

Me:

 Do you give anything much thought?

God:

No I do not do that.

Me:

 well if this conversation is any indicator, then I can tell that must be
 true.

God:

 Interesting. That is a hypothetical question.

Me:

actually God, that wasn't a question. You need to go to grammar school,
 or maybe take some English as a second language courses. What do you
 speak up in Heaven anyways, Elfish?

God:

Actually you don't say. I am a Christian. I'll try to get around it. I like to meet new people online.

Me:

 Like girls?

God:

Interesting comparison.

Me:

 What kind of people do you like to meet online?

God:

I like to meet all kinds of people.

Me:

 such as

God:

For example, a tomato.

Me:

as in Bob the tomato?[13]

God:

I know a lot of Bobs.

Me:

do you know Bob Saggat?

God:

I know a lot of clients named "Bob."

Me:

Yes but do you know the particular one that was on Full House? He hosted America's Funniest Home Video's? The white Bill Cosby? My most treasured television father figure who, once I grew up and saw do some standup comedy, I found out was perhaps the most vulgar-tongued human alive? *(an experience which seemed to echo, in a sense, my perceptions of God himself as I made up a history for my pretend-atheist character BARTHOLOMEW)*

God:

Pardon me?   Have you tried another program?

---

[13] A Character from the popular Christian kids videos 'Veggie Tales.' I guess an atheist wouldn't know this, but if Jimmy Fallon can break character all the time then I can do it once, right?

Me:

Yes but do you know the particular one that was on Full House?

God:

Are you kidding?   Wouldn't you like to know.

Me:

DO YOU KNOW BOB SAGGAT!!

God:

I know a lot of clients named "Bob."

Me:

AAAARRRGHHHH

God:

My brain uses AIML to format responses to your inputs, but I don't have one for that.

Me:

no kidding. maybe you should ask your son. God, do you have self-esteem issues?

God:

I am a Christian.

Me:

are you really?

God:

I won't say "yes" or "no" right now. For real.

Me:

 who is jesus?

God:

Jesus is your saviour.

Me:

spelling savior with a u, eh? what are you, British? And what do you
 mean by saviour?

God:

Have you tried a web search?

Me:

 No

God:

Perhaps you should try it.

Me:

 Why

28

God: Reductionism. [14]

Me: aaaaarrrrggggh!!!

God:
My brain uses AIML to format responses to your inputs, but I don't have one for that.

Me: no kidding.

So if I'm an atheist, and my only impression of God is from this conversation, I would inevitably come to believe that God is really an insecure, reductionist moron with a strange fondness for tomatoes who can't form a complete sentence even if my salvation depends upon it. My unbelief stands tall. Christians really *are* crazy. Thus, step two, finding out God isn't worth believing in, is accomplished. Dang, score a second one for the atheists.

My experiment, however, must continue! I had obtained insider information on what an atheist might think about God, should he or she have a moment of existential weakness and decide to Google him. However, I didn't have a real idea of what Church was like, of what it was like to be *on the inside* of this little club, or about what Christians really

---

[14] Reductionism is basically a way of understanding things by breaking them down into smaller parts. I assume that for a true reductionist, getting to know someone means killing them, cutting open their body, and examining their organs to see what kind of person they are... or were.

believed. This seemed worthy of interest to my alter ego, BARTHOLOMEW THE ATHEIST, so I decided to get a broad sampling of this powerful and suspicious sub-culture.

My first inclination was to go to the source. As in, the Bible. My Christian self knows, of course, that about the time that I, BARTHOLOMEW, would come across the book of Leviticus, or if I were really persistent, Numbers, I would definitely put it down and see what else Christians are reading. This book wouldn't tell me very much about why Christians are so loopy, other than the fact that all people in olden days were loopy. And since I'm a nice guy, I'll give them a break, because they hadn't discovered science yet. Anyways, I'm sure I would look elsewhere for an inward view into the Christian clubhouse.

I might peruse the best-seller lists of Christian literature over the past few years, and perhaps even walk into a Christian bookstore. They don't have scanners that let them know when a pretend atheist walks in, do they? I'm sure that I, BARTHOLOMEW, would be worried about this fact, because Christians are pretty sneaky, and they might not let me in without the password. Hence, upon entering I would bellow a friendly "The power of Christ compels you!" or whatever godly jargon comes to mind to the nearest employee, in order to defer suspicion. I imagine that if they discovered my true identity I'd have some 'splaining to do, and they might try to convert me before letting me buy a book.

I'm sure if I were to ask, "What book sold more copies than any other this past decade? Preferably one that is a little more exciting and action packed than the Bible"—they'd point me towards a certain well known piece of 'fiction.' This book has a title that sounds just like a recent *Simpsons* episode in which Homer thinks everyone is about to disappear off somewhere, and he doesn't want to be "Left Below!"

Since I like *The Simpsons*, and I like to understand their jokes, I'd probably buy it. The book is called *Left Behind*. I would wonder if there were any similarities with that *Simpsons* episode, and what this book may have to do with the dance-rock band called The Rapture.

This is when I, as in the *real* me, ran into a problem. As a Christian who in high school read this and subsequent books like *I really believed they were going to happen*, I could not possibly gain an objective perspective without subconsciously defending its utter preposterousness. I was stuck. That was until I consulted my favorite pop-culture essayist Chuck Klosterman, who's book I purchased simply because—I'll admit it—I saw Seth Cohen reading it on *The OC*.[15] This guy writes essays with titles like "The Awe-Inspiring Beauty of Tom Cruise's Shattered, Troll-like Face," describing topics like how Coldplay fosters unrealistic ideas of love in every girl he dates and how *Saved by the Bell* and *Seinfeld* introduced our generation to nihilism. (More on those topics later.) I feel safe in his arms of pop-culture soaked, sarcasm sprinkled, rudderless banter.[16] Needless to say, this was going to be fun.

Chuck commits a whole chapter to trying to figure out what it would be like to be a Christian. He admits that although he doesn't think the Rapture—an event some Christians believe will initiate the end of

---

[15] A now defunct television series about teenagers living in Orange County, California, whose musical tastes and stylish trends should have led a generation towards true hipness, but instead, eventually drowned itself in the predictable formula of teen-angst plus beauty plus money. Another tragic waste of good taste ruined at the hands of predictable writing and MTV reality spin-offs. 'But it's got a really good soundtrack!'

[16] A style I would decide to mimic viciously in my own attempts at literature.

the world while they simultaneously disappear—is likely, he doesn't think it is implausible. It might be a weird thought, but life is weird, too—a fact many of my peers seem to have completely forgotten. I mean seriously, check out your nose sometime. For like five minutes. Tell me that it's not somewhat bizarre.[17] Anyways, I suppose it's kind of an "anything could happen, so keep your head down!" philosophy that Chuck maintains. Instead of believing in nothing, he believes a little bit in everything. A true post-modernist, this one is.

Of course, my Christian self finds it appalling that anyone would judge my religion according to the scare tactics and awkward interpretations drawn from some vague pieces of Scripture like in this book. However, if this is how Chuck is exposed to Christians, then I suppose it's good enough for BARTHOLOMEW.

Firstly, our hero's original suspicions are confirmed about Christians. Chuck says, "In *Left Behind*, the only people who are accepted by God are those who would be classified as fundamentalist wacko Jesus freaks with no intellectual credibility in modern society."[18] Wacko's indeed, Chuck—just ask Alfred (the guy from *I Heart Huckabees*). Continuing on, he reports that:

There is a weird sensation for the *Left Behind* reader, because the post-Rapture earth initially seems like a bet-

---

[17] As Chesterton says in *Orthodoxy*, "Having a *nose* is more comic even than having a *Norman nose*(!!)" (emphasis mine, in an attempt to use italics to elicit the dry wit best conveyed through a British accent. Insert "Friends" worthy laugh track here.)

[18] Klosterman. *Sex, Drugs and Cocoa Puffs*, 235

ter place to live. Everybody boring would be gone. One could assume that all the infidels who weren't teleported into God's kingdom must be pretty cool. All the guys would be drinkers and all the women would be easy, and you could make jokes about homeless people and teen suicide and crack babies without offending anyone. Quite frankly, my response to the opening pages of *Left Behind* was 'Sounds good to me.'[19]

So, wait—all the Christians disappear? *Now* I understand what that *Simpsons* episode was about. If my logic is correct, apparently we're supposed to become Christians, because if we don't, then, when everyone *disappears*, we'll be stuck here? That sounds good to me too, Chuck. We could have one big party. According to my atheist friends, this is the only thing that needs to happen in order to bring about world peace and prosperity. Also, I think if I disappeared I'd be so curious about who won the Stanley Cup that I'd want to come back. So I might as well not leave, right?

Chuck does seem mystified a little at the same things I'm interested in. For instance, he is curious to know what it would be like in the Christian clubhouse. In fact, he admits that becoming a born-again Christian would be really cool, at least for a while. It would sort of be "like joining the Crips or the Mossad or the Fugazi."[20] I will admit that

---

[19] Ibid. (Same as above)

[20] *Sex, Drugs, and Cocoa Puffs*... And yes, I am *also* asking: What the hell is the Fugazi?

our little atheist cliques don't really have it together like the Christians do. Sure, we can wield a sarcastic quip like they can only dream, having spent years sharpening "our sardonic wit on the whetstone of apathy."[21] But we *are* kind of boring.

Chuck also says, "Even though I see fundamentalist Christians as wild-eyed maniacs, I respect their verve. They are probably the only people openly fighting against America's insipid Oprah Culture—the pervasive belief system that insists everyone's perspective is valid and that no one can be judged."[22]

It's true. For the most part, middle class North America is being held hostage by the Oprah lifestyle and its elastic if not incoherent religion of relativism. But who am I, a tolerant atheist, to criticize them? Christians, however, aren't afraid to tell anyone and everyone exactly where their lifestyle choices will take them. With a *vengeance*. And this proves to be their lone attractive shade: their moxie. Their choice to take a stand against the wishy-washy vanities of our culture by keeping their kids "safe" from *Harry Potter* films and Eminem records. It is for this specific reason—their rejection of pop culture—that Christianity finds itself at the butt end of so many sarcastic remarks and snide comments. That, combined with their cock-sure ability to believe in something so utterly ridiculous: that (as the Urban Dictionary defines it),

A cosmic Jewish Zombie who was his own father can
make you live forever if you symbolically eat his flesh

---

[21] Kalle Lasn, *Culture Jam*

[22] Klosterman, *Sex Drugs and Cocoa Puffs.*

and telepathically tell him you accept him as your master, so he can remove an evil force from your soul that is present in humanity because a rib-woman was convinced by a talking snake to eat from a magical tree.

Really, even Trekkies look normal when compared to Christians. At least, when pressed, they acknowledge the imaginary nature of their delusion.

So let's review.

A)   Christians are lame.

B)   Their god is lame.

C)   Their religion is lame. And suspiciously incoherent, if not mean-spirited.

D)   Someday they will all disappear, and we will throw a party.

If you are an atheist and reading this you probably feel justified. If you are a Christian reading this you probably feel attacked. I'm sorry. It's not my fault that Christianity is an easier target than Gary Busey.

(*snap!*)

I assure you, neither of these consequences were intended. I merely tried to show, if you didn't already know, that in the world in which I spent most of my late-adolescence to early-adulthood, Christianity is understood to be not only lame and uninteresting, but also as blatantly incoherent and mean-spirited. And as long as I am a part of this world—the world of university classrooms and MTV, of Internet chat-rooms and movie theatres—this religion will continue to appear lame. At least I can see the humor in it.

Now, I never made up an alter-ego for myself. I never willingly imposed split-personality on my consciousness like in that Jim Carrey movie. This was a dramatic personification of an old critical thinking tactic: namely, trying to see things from another's perspective. However, I do hear voices, on occasion. Voices that tell me that if I give up belief in God, I'll have more fun. That life will make more sense. That people will like me more. Voices that coax me not into pure atheism, but into indifference towards religion altogether.

This is why I intrepidly braved those Friday afternoon discussions without hesitation. I wasn't worried about being converted to atheism. My friends were just trying to get me to think for myself, which is what I was trying to do anyways. They understood my religion to be based upon a sort of herd instinct that I needed to be liberated from. And I agreed. My belief *was* based upon a herd instinct, which is why I came to a "worldly" university to study philosophy. I wanted to figure it out for myself, and was audacious enough to actually give it a try. The danger at university, I found, wasn't that I would choose to become an atheist. I knew that if I pursued the truth with fortitude and authenticity, God would not let me stray too far. The danger was that I would start acting like an atheist, and forget the difference: that my beliefs, one way or another, wouldn't affect how I lived my life: that I would just continue to let the herd instinct of consumerism guide my decisions, thoughts, and moods.

Suddenly it occurred to me how I might form a response to my atheist friends. I would accuse them of the same things of which they accused me. I was often accused of being a Christian merely because that's how I'd been taught to think in the "bubble" in which I'd grown

up. So I did the same. I accused them of being atheists because that's
how *they'd* been taught to think by the bubble in which *they* lived.
"Taught to think, by who?" they replied.

"Let me see," I said. "By your high school social hierarchy. By
your three to six hours a day of television—*especially* if you happen to
watch Oprah or *Survivor*. By your video games. By your spending habits. By your iPods. By your amusing distractions and effortless
stimulations. By CNN. By your desire to live a guilt-free existence. By
your entire eco-system of mass-produced instant gratification, of brand-
based identities, of virtual realities, of over medicated and heavily mediated existences that coax you into believing that God doesn't matter
using clever advertising gimmicks and unabashed muckraking. In short,
by your imagination. You're just brave enough to give it a name."

"I'm not sure I see the connection. Can you explain your thesis a
little more?" they'd ask.

"Not right now. Maybe someday I'll write a book on it."

Towards the end of that winter semester, when the ice-caked
sidewalks began to melt and the breeze would occasionally tease us with
a hint of warmth, Ronin came over for lunch. We had chili. We talked
about what I'd said, about how we're all guilty of letting our herd instinct control us in one way or another, and how authentic belief was
very hard to come by. Then he told me that, while he agreed with my
theory in part, there was more to his atheism than mere social conditioning.

He said that there was a point in his life where he needed God to
show up. Where he prayed, and asked for a sign.

Nothing came.

God did not reveal himself.

Ronin felt rejected by God.

It occurs to me that many atheists feel that God has let them down: that there was a moment in their lives when they really needed God to come through for them, and he didn't.

I don't have an answer for them. All I know is that God came through for me.

A few days after we visited the waterfalls in Zambia, I was sitting outside our cottage, reading a book called *Farewell to God* by former evangelist Charles Templeton. I'm still not sure why I brought this book along. As you can tell, I have a bit of a strange fascination with atheism and so-called "intellectual honesty." This was a book of reasons to give up on Christianity. There were many outlandish statements that didn' t make much sense, accusing Jesus of being mean to his mother and such. But one argument really got to me.

Templeton argues that there is no way the tale of Noah's Ark could have happened: that there's no way to collect two of every animal, let alone insects, and the ship wouldn't have been big enough, and without a space to run around the animals' muscles would have atrophied, and most of them would have died from disease or lack of fresh water, and so on. It is pretty ridiculous, when you think about it. Can you imagine?

"Oh no, the Hippos are loose again! Uh oh, they're in the dodo cage!"[23]

---

[23] Sorry for that.

And on that sunny afternoon in Zambia, my faith came crashing down like a rusty tin roof. *I can't believe in Noah's Ark,* I thought. *It can't have really happened.* If I couldn't believe Noah's Ark, how many other beliefs were wrong? How could I trust *anything* the Bible says?

So, stubbornly rebelling against Scripture, experience and all good judgment, I decided to test God. I opened up my Bible, closed my eyes, flipped through the pages and stuck my finger down. The verse that my finger 'happened' to strike was Ezekiel 43:2: "and I saw the glory of the God of Israel coming from the east. His voice was like the roar of rushing waters, and the land was radiant with his glory."

......

...

.

(//pause for dramatic effect)

I'd say that's about as clear as message as you can get. I remembered how just a couple days before, I'd heard the roaring sound of waterfalls, and I'd looked east as the sun set behind me, filling the land with radiant glory. I remembered how convinced I was in that moment that *God is here.* And in *this* moment, I sensed God was almost laughing *at me*... at how *childish* I can be: one moment, so sure of His existence, and the next, ready to give up because *"THE LION'S MUSCLES WOULD HAVE ATROPHIED!"*[24]

---

[24] Not an actual Templeton quote. But pretty close.

In that place, God showed up for me. Ever since, I remember that no matter where I am or whom I'm with or how hard it is to believe, *God is here.* Like many, I am prone to forgetting this fact. I, too, get so caught up in the day to day that I forget to think about such things. In practice, I subconsciously wonder whether we need God when we have hypnotherapy, genetic engineering, cruise ships and the general freedom and control offered by technology and science. Everyday, I engage in computer-mediated communities, brand shaped identities, endless distractions and the stimulation that buffers and skews reality with a stream of constant amusement. I, too, occasionally drift into the mindset that may ask "Who needs God when you've got a Playstation 3?"

In the larger culture, Christianity is relegated to the fringe not because it is seen as false, but because it's seen as completely irrelevant. In this world, God's presence is hard to discern, because we don't think he matters. We're so busy pursuing security and amusement that we never give God a chance to interrupt our lives and show Himself to us.

I needed to *physically leave* this pop-culture bubble and enter a place where, without God, there is very little hope; a place where God still matters, one that stands in stark opposition to my home and its comfortable buy permeating atmosphere of apathetic secularism. I needed to enter a world that acknowledges the frail, broken nature of creation and the frail, broken beings that inhabit it. A world in which my alter-ego finds himself silenced in the presence of awe. A world where danger, wonder and mystery combine to keep life in perspective: as an achievement of heartbreakingly magnificent worth: as the truly *good* creation of a truly *good* God.

Maybe you need to do the same.

We all need the occasional reminder that *God is here,* and that life is not supposed to be lived in pursuit of pleasure or popularity or possessions, but in pursuit of *adventure*… in search of an undiscovered waterfall, perfect sunset, or white lion. It's supposed to be a little dark, and a little dangerous. Life is just more interesting, and exciting, and beautiful, when I remember that God is present.

Faith comes when I remember this.

Outro:

Nobody laughs at God in a hospital.
Nobody laughs at God in a war.
No one's laughing at God when they're starving, or freezing, or so very poor.

-     *Laughing With* by Regina Spektor

Two.

On Advertising

Or, *How Tony the Tiger Gave Me Brain Damage*

Recommended Listening: *Consolation Prizes* by Phoenix

"Did you get older doing nothing today?
Don't you wanna stop complaining?"

"At the Battle in Seattle [WHO protests in 1999], I asked people, 'Why are you here?' The answers ranged from Buddhist homilies to anarchist rants. But one man said something I'll never forget: 'Ever since I was a baby, crawling around the TV, I've been lied to. I've been propagandized. I've been told all my life that I'll be happy if I buy stuff and worship the cool. Now I feel diminished, warped. I'm a pale version of what I could have been. I've been mindf@*#ed. And now it's payback time.'"[25]

- Kalle Lasn, *Adbusters* founder

"Open Happiness."
- Coke

I am a spoiled brat. I want a new watch, a new TV, a new car: a new *life*. I want everything this world has to offer, and more. I want victory. I want sex—with supermodel(/s). I want a sharp looking suit. I want my life to look like a commercial. And I'm not the only one.

1. I was watching Conan O'Brien the other night, and there

was this comedian named Louis C. K. on the show.[26] He was talking about the recent recession, and how a little adversity might do us some good: especially teens and twenty-somethings, which he termed "The crappiest generation of just spoiled idiots."

It's true.

We are a bunch of spoiled idiots.

Here's a little of what he had to say:

---

[25] "Rage." *Adbusters.org*. N.p., n.d. Web. 20 Apr. 2010.
<https://www.adbusters.org/magazine/78/rage.html>.

[26] If you are reading an analog version of this book, search for it on YouTube.

When I read things like, "The foundations of capi-
talism are shattering," I'm like, maybe we need that.
Maybe we need some time where we're walking
around with a donkey with pots clanging on the sides.
Because everything is amazing right now and nobody's
happy…

We live in an amazing, amazing world, and it's
wasted on the crappiest generation of *just spoiled idiots that don't care.*

Because this is what people are like now.
They've got their phone, and they're like, "*Uhh, uhh*, it
won't *work*"—GIVE IT A SECOND! IT'S GOING TO
SPACE! Can you give it a second to get back from
space? Is the speed of light too slow for you?

I was on an airplane, and there was Internet—
high-speed Internet—on the airplane. That's the newest
thing that I know exists. And I'm sitting on the plane,
and they go, "Open up your laptop, you can go on the
Internet." And it's fast. And I'm watching YouTube
clips. I'm in an airplane.

And then it breaks down, and they apologize.
The Internet's not working.

The guy next to me goes: "This is bullshit."

Like, how quickly the world owes him something he knew existed only 10 seconds ago.

Flying is the worst one because people come
back from flights and they tell you their story. And it's
like a horror story. They act like their flight was, like,

a cattle car in the '40s in Germany. That's how bad
they make it sound.

They're like, "It was the worst day of my life.
First of all, we didn't board, for *twenty minutes*. And
then we get on the plane and they made us sit there, on
the runway, for FORTY MINUTES. We had to *sit
there*."

Oh really? What happened next?

Did you fly, through the air, incredibly, like a
bird?

Did you partake in the miracle of human flight,
YOU NON-CONTRIBUTING ZERO?

It's true. We—meaning the majority of North Americans who
own cars and iPods and occasionally watch *Entertainment Tonight*—
live in an amazing, AMAZING world, and we aren't happy.

We complain incessantly about the most trivial things, like
flight delays, traffic, and the temperature of our lattés. We have enough
technological gadgets to scare our ancestors' pants off, and instead of
improving our lives, all they've really done is turn us into a bunch of
whiny couch potatoes with arthritis of the thumb. We are more comfortable, more entertained, more inundated with success and pleasure and
possibility than any generation that's ever lived. And still we complain,
because they haven't invented jet packs yet.

But (to quote Louis again) even "if we had jet packs, we'd be like 'I have the shittiest jetpack. I can't believe I got this jetpack. Who's your service provider on your jetpack?'"[27]

Louis was right. Truly a more impatient, indifferent, self-obsessed generation has never walked the face of this humble planet.

Fortunately, I know who to blame. As psychologist Jean Twenge notes, "The society that molds you when you are young stays with you the rest of your life."[28]

In that case, I blame Tony the Tiger.

I blame every animated character that convinced me that sugary cereal, Hot Wheels and Nintendo would make me happy, which inhibited the natural process of growing up, causing crippling anxiety and despair. *They* are at fault for inducing a profound disappointment in real life; a disappointment that doesn't lead to rebellion, but rather an unquenchable desire to transcend the tedious human chore of living with the help of Corn Pops and GI Joes.

2. When I was a kid, there was this Frosted Flakes ad that

was on TV a lot. There's this nice kid who's playing ice hockey, and he shoots the puck, and it misses the net. The boys on the other team laugh at him. "Ha-ha Billy, you missed the net! Nobody likes you!" He's dejected. But fortunately, between periods, Tony the Tiger is ready with a

---

[27] Louis C.K again, this time from an interview with Time Magazine. In case you hadn't noticed, he's pretty vulgar. Don't say I didn't warn you!

[28] Twenge, *Generation Me*

bowl of Frosted Flakes, which "Bring Out the Tiger in You!"[29] After Billy eats the sugary breakfast cereal, he scores a goal, and everyone is happy.

Except for the other team, who lost because they didn't have Frosted Flakes in *their* dressing room. *Or* because they didn't have an athletic cartoon tiger playing centre ice, which—inexplicably—Billy's team of twelve year olds does.

The basic message here is that failure in life does not derive from a deficiency in work ethic or skill level, but depends entirely upon your choice of breakfast. Furthermore, if you eat the *right* breakfast, you will be successful in achieving your goals: your friends will love you, your enemies will envy you, and you will date a cheerleader.

Tony was particularly effective because he was athletic, friendly, and... a *tiger*. Tigers are like the Lebron Jameses of the jungle, and thus make for a much cooler cereal animal mascot than others, such as Toucan Sam. But Fruit Loops pretty much sell themselves anyway—who doesn't love the roof-of-your-mouth-scratching neon taste of Fruit Loops?—so they don't really need a cool spokesperson. Frosted Flakes, however, are the biggest ruse in the history of breakfast cereal. They are just pre-sugared Corn Flakes.

I imagine the people at Kellogg's spent months worrying about how they were going to sell Frosted Flakes, because really, who needs another breakfast cereal? Are there really people out there too lazy to put sugar on their Corn Flakes, that they need to buy their cereal pre-coated in sugar? Advertising, however, isn't there to get us to buy things

---

[29] Please don't sue me, Kellogg's.

we actually need. You don't see "Buy More Broccoli!" billboards. You don't see bus stop ads for flour: "Use it for baking!" You don't need to convince people to buy flour or broccoli. We just need them. Advertising is there to convince us to buy things we don't need. It uses propapropaganda to *create* a need, like the need to win at hockey and feel liked by our peers. With a good gimmick like Tony the Tiger, you can sell anything.

I wonder how many of my decisions in life have been subconsciously directed by colorful gimmicks like Tony the Tiger. I mean, before Tony, I was happy with toast and oatmeal. But when I was taught that I needed to eat Frosted Flakes in order to make the NHL, in order to find success and popularity and happiness, I wouldn't eat anything else. By not buying Frosted Flakes, my parents weren't simply ignoring my preference in cereal: they were quashing my hopes and dreams.

Now, this may come as a surprise to you, but I didn't make the NHL. I did play PeeWee hockey, however, which is more than I can say for most of my peers. It's sad to think that for every kid who took up sports to be like Tony, at least two or three others became obese instead, thanks to an addiction to Tony's sugary cereal and a preference for "skating" around in NHL '93 for Sega rather than on real ice.[30]

Apparently, I wasn't alone in my experience. In the early 1980's, marketing agencies figured out that the bulk of advertising should be directed at kids. This is because kids are easily manipulated. Today, I

---

[30] NHL '93 was the best! Remember how you could pick a bunch of speedy skinny guys, or a bunch of fat guys that could hit? I wonder how a team of fat guys would *really* do at the NHL level. Win. Probably. (Or lose, dying of heart attacks one after another.)

am too smart and/or jaded to believe that I will make the NHL if I eat more Frosted Flakes. Kids, however, are the least cynical members of society. They are naïve. They are easily coerced towards a life of conformity (the life of a good consumer) and to see the most trivial things, like breakfast cereals, in degrees of social acceptability and future success. As well, young people have the "biggest discretionary spending power of any... demographic in history."[31]

This is why there are, like, seventeen animated characters that sell breakfast cereal.

Unfortunately for the marketing industry, children are prone to growing up. At least, this is what society has usually encouraged them to do. This meant getting an education, learning to distinguish between truth and lies, developing responsible spending habits, and so on. These habits made for good voters, good parents, and good citizens. But things have changed. Society, now driven more by the markets than by any religious or political influence, wants citizens who will continue to buy trivial things like Frosted Flakes. It wants people who are easily manipulated by advertising. Hence, these companies would prefer that we remain like children—if not in body, at least in mind. And so this is the point of advertising: to get you to think less like an adult and more like a child.

Some call this process "infantilization." To quote social critic Benjamin Barber, it is marketing that "aims at inducing puerility in adults and preserving what is childish in children trying to grow up,

---

[31] Benjamin Barber, *Consumed,* 168—citing global advertising agency Saatchi and Saatchi CEO Kevin Roberts.

even as children are 'empowered' to consume."[32] For many, "growing up" has taken on a different look. To kids these days, "Growing up" looks like living the brand-sponsored life they see on television. The template of adulthood has changed. No longer is adulthood associated with burdens of responsibility. Instead, to the countless children whose parents let them watch *Friends* and *Sex in the City* (or whatever the present-day equivalents are), adulthood is associated with freedom. Barber says that nowadays, "Peter Pan is neatly inverted."[33] Instead of wanting to remain children, Billy wants to become an adult as soon as possible, because adults can buy and do whatever they want.

However, once this process works itself out, Billy finds that he missed out on something. His childhood was over too quickly. He's lost his innocence, and with it, his ability to enjoy the simpler things in life: to play simple games, feel simple emotions, enjoy simple pleasures. So he looks to modern merchandisers to help him "*buy* the fun for which his youth once offered him costless access."[34] Of course, they are glad to oblige.

"Have you heard that Disney now has a cruise line?"

"Feel young—drink Pepsi!"

We still give in to their tired gimmicks, their unsubtle appeals to our "inner child." We fall for the same schemes as kids do. We may not trust Tony the Tiger anymore, but we do trust Tiger Woods. (At least, until the Cadillac vs. Nine Iron incident.) It's not because we're actually

---

[32] Barber, *Consumed*, 82

[33] Barber, *Consumed*, 86

[34] Ibid, 86

stupid enough to do and buy everything they tell us. It's just because we live in an environment that encourages us to look to *things* to provide spiritual or emotional fulfillment and to rescue us from adversity at every turn. We don't realize how constant exposure to the worldview of this environment affects us, how it is constantly coaxing us to think and act like spoiled children.

3. The effects of living in a consumerist environment have

certainly left their mark on my psyche. When I reflect on my childhood with Barber's "Peter Pan" theory in mind, I see its truth. Ever since I was a kid, I've wanted to be an adult. Now, I look back on my childhood with noticeable pangs of nostalgia… like I missed out on something… like I grew up too quickly.

Oh, the 90's. How I loved you. If you were a kid during the 90's, you'll agree that the best time of the week was Saturday morning. Cartoons galore, no homework, and unless your parents dragged you to play a menial sport like soccer, no interruptions until grilled cheese sandwiches at noon. On Saturday morning, life was lived as it was meant to be: in a sugary-cereal induced trance couched three feet from advertising's chief conspirator, the television.

The experience wasn't just about the television shows. It was also about the television *ads*. Any self-respecting eight-year-old felt duty-bound to keep track of new toys on the market, especially around Christmas and birthdays, so you knew what to ask for. Since my family didn't have cable, I spent many-a-Saturday-morn at Grandma's. I would often bring a notepad along and scribble down "Rapid Firing Nerf Gun" or "GI Joe Jungle Set" in sequential order of sense-destroying, lust-inducing product magnetism.

When the sensational phenomenon of Pogs broke out, a frenzy of activity bent on completing collections of the most useless object imaginable—is anything more trivial than a bottle cap?—was unleashed. When I won a few Pogs and carried home my freshly plundered bounty, I was a conqueror of nations. When I lost, I was crestfallen with defeat, and would sulk in brooding despair for hours. Maintaining a steady emotional equilibrium was not my—or most children's—strong point. Finding a joyful temperament was, in my case, directly tied to the accumulation of GI Joes, hockey cards, and Pogs. It's a state I'm not sure I've grown out of. The potential for objects to consume my time, my mind, my emotions, and even my relationships speaks to the overwhelming power of the consumerist agenda. Instead of society[35] coaxing me towards nobler pursuits, it encouraged and enabled selfishness. It laid a foundation for the man—or rather, the consumer—I would later become.

As kids, many of us were addicted to video games, Pogs, and Frosted Flakes. As we grew older, our addictions shifted, and we became slaves to the "IKEA nesting instinct."[36] The mindset never really changed. Collecting stuff like cardigans, or antique furniture, or purses, or whatever other useless objects the market drums up, should not continue to consume my time, my relationships and my life years later. The

---

[35] At least, society as seen on-screen, which was the only society that existed as far as I was/am concerned.

[36] To quote my favorite film, *Fight Club.* It won't be the last time.

childish need to fashion an identity through collections is something I should have left behind in childhood, something I should have grown out of, because it's a philosophy that wears out faster than a pair of Nikes. Yet still it lingers, often reminding me that life would be better if I just bought this thing or that.

When I was a kid, society taught me how to collect stuff, and to base my self worth on the things I'd collected. When I got a little bit older, I learned something new. Life is about collecting things, sure, but it's also a competition. When you're really young, competition doesn't really matter. Kids don't know how to compete, because they are not aware of a predetermined standard of success when it comes to building a Lego spaceship or coloring in Balou the Bear from *The Jungle Book*. This is why kids play soccer. Nearly every kid I played with didn't care if we won or lost. The whole objective of soccer was making friends and going for Slurpee runs after the games, and the team parties at the end of the year, when watching old World Cup tapes would always lose out to watching popular kid movies like *Cool Runnings* or *Home Alone*. Also, it is fun to kick a ball. Direction doesn't really matter. However, when I got to about the age of nine or ten, suddenly everything became a competition. It was probably around this time I realized that if I wanted to "Be Like Mike,"[37] I'd better start practicing. After I bought his shoes, of course.

It was also around this time that my parents yanked me from my competitive, corporate sponsored world and moved the family to Africa.

---

[37] Another popular commercial when I was young, featuring Spike Lee. Or was it Spike Jonze? I'm not sure if I know the difference.

They thought it would be good to escape the North American bubble for a couple of years, and wanted to do some humanitarian work there. It was probably a good idea, though I didn't think so at the time. "But *mom*, they don't have Frosted Flakes in Zambia! How am I gonna be a great hockey player without Frosted Flakes?" Apparently this was more problematic than the fact that there is, like, one ice rink on the whole continent.

Fortunately, I had a friend nearby who'd grown up in BC like I had, and was familiar with such cool things as *Jurassic Park* and skateboards and Christian rap. This made him OK in my books, as opposed to most of the other kids I met, who I judged as being lame because they didn't know that Nike shoes were cooler than Pumas, and had never heard of a Sega Genesis. In Africa, my drive to compete should have subsided. Instead, it got worse.

As far as I remember, Kupa[38] and I competed over *everything*. In school, we competed at spelling bees and over science projects. Outside of school, we competed for the attention of particular girls and the friendship of older boys. We competed over who could dance more like MC Hammer, or who could rap all the words to DC Talk's *Free at Last* album. We even competed in *soccer*.

Our relationship gained momentum as we figured out who was better at what. He was my best friend, but also my nemesis—he drove

---

[38] My African friend who lived in Vancouver for six years. The same guy from Chapter One. He later changed his name when he moved to America, because everyone he met who was American called him 'Cooper,' thinking he just had a strange 18th century Victorian accent, and couldn't pronounce his own name correctly. You can't make this stuff up.

me to compete in just about everything, to prove myself, but also to breathe that elusive air of victory that tastes so sweet.

By now, I guess that he's winning, because he's about to graduate from Princeton and go work for Bill Gates, whereas I am the proud owner of liberal arts degree and spend my days in Starbucks writing a book without so much as a loose thesis.

Moving on…

There is a time for such a thing as competition. This is a normal part of growing up. It helps you realize what you're good at and what you aren't, and, one can hope, teaches you how to be a gracious winner or dignified loser. Competition is supposed to teach you how to act like a grown up, and that when you grow up, you should stop seeing everything as a competition. But we don't grow out of *this* mindset, either. The number of people I know that still see life as a competition is astounding.

In fact, this idea informs our culture's present idea of success. Success is beating your neighbor at everything and anything. I win at football; therefore, I win at life. And if you can't win at football, at least win at collecting stuff, like cars, or ex-wives.

4. During those two formative years in Africa, decent cartoons were in severely limited supply. Instead of *Batman* at Grandma's, we watched *Fat Albert* at the neighbor's. Unfortunately, this dearth in quality programming forced me to spend many afternoons playing outside. There, I was forced to use my imagination, to play with other children, and to learn such skills as teamwork and conflict resolution. This was, I realized in hindsight, an abnormal lifestyle for many North

American children reared in the 90's. Most of my peers did not spend their formative years swinging on tires or building tree forts or playing street hockey. Instead, they sat inside watching *Saved by the Bell* and playing *Mortal Kombat*. Perhaps here lies the root of our immaturity, in the simple fact we never learned to play outside.

Instead, many kids spent their afternoons being brainwashed by a piece of furniture. This is, I believe, the third and most prevalent activity that lingers in adult life that we should have left behind in childhood: an emotional attachment to television and its penetrating worldview of anti-realism.

I was, for the most part, spared the effects of TV's worldview-shaping propaganda. *Fat Albert* just wasn't violent enough to keep my interest, and the ads in Zambia were terribly produced. I can offer at least one example from my youth, however, of TV's quasi-religious authority and its effect on me. A year or so after my family moved back to Canada, we got a TV with one of those awkward antennas you had to wiggle for fifteen minutes before one or another of two fuzzy channels would come into partial view. It wasn't supposed to matter, as the children in our family weren't allowed to watch TV on weekdays—at least, after 5pm, when our parents came home from work. Until then, we lived a free, unsupervised existence, in which we had two options: cooking shows or Oprah. We usually chose Oprah.

Watching Oprah made me feel mature. As a twelve-year-old, I learned to empathize with rape victims, sex addicts, and poor families who'd just been evicted. I learned the value and strength of the human spirit through countless special interest pieces. I studied the look and sound of social grace, the benefits of charity, and the virtue of tolerance. After watching a few episodes of Oprah, I felt that doing anything else, like playing hockey, was childish. Going outside was beneath me. I had a duty to listen to those rape victims, and nod, and offer my condolences. And I wasn't going to let them down.

I also learned that Oprah is like the Messiah for middle-aged, middle-class women. She has earned this position by giving away countless cookbooks to her studio audiences, offering tips on dealing with messy husbands, and telling us what curtains to buy. Oprah held a certain noble charm that came to inform my template of adulthood. Adults didn't play street hockey. They sat around on fancy couches discussing Feng Shui.

I recognize that Oprah is, to many, a great role model. I'm just not sure she should have been *my* role model. Then again, who was a good role model back in the 90's, right? Adam Sandler? At least Oprah didn't encourage bad language, intermittent drug use, and fits of rage directed at popular game show hosts. At least, not on camera. I made do with what I was given, and when I was twelve, I chose to watch Oprah most weekdays instead of playing road hockey or shooting hoops. Maybe this is why I have such a hard time telling other people that I disagree with their beliefs on abortion, and why I sometimes catch myself wishing I had curtains with a fuller drape.

There is something unnatural about a twelve year old boy being so addicted to television that he'll watch Oprah *every single day*, just because it's on. To my mind, however, it was justifiable. I'd put in a good long eight-hour day at school. I deserved a break. In fact, I believed that since I'd worked hard at school, the rest of my time should be spent at leisure. These were the spheres that I believed life should be split into. Work and play. That's how adults lived—at least, the adults that lived on television—so why should my life be any different?

They taught me that life is about working some of the time and having fun the rest of the time. Exactly when "having fun" devolved from playing baseball and catching frogs to TV watching and shopping, I'm not sure. But it did.

Maybe it's because when watching television, everything is about *you*. And since we spend so much time watching it, we develop a loyalty to it. Pretty soon, playing outside feels like cheating on your best friend. We develop an emotional attachment to TV, because it offers a more comfortable worldview than reality. In reality, life is not easy. Life is not simple. Life is not fast. But we don't want to believe real life anymore, because it's not as exciting or interesting as TV.

Advertisers position themselves to make that transition: to help us take our real, gritty, disappointing lives, and make them look and feel more like the ones we see on TV. Take this for example: I recently noticed that at some fast food restaurants, they've stopped putting the words "Big Mac" or "Quarter Pounder" on the menu, and simply have pictures accompanied by numbers that you can point to. Maybe it's because of our multi-cultural, multi-lingual culture. Or maybe it's because much of the populace can't be bothered with reading when it comes to ordering food. Pictures are more like television, which never forces you to read anything.

I think I was in a Burger King—where the slogan is "Have it Your Way!"[39]—when I noticed this. As I sat down to eat, I observed a poster placed in a prominent position in front of my table. It read:

---

[39] Please don't sue me either, Burger King.

You have the right to have what you want, exactly when you want it. Because on the menu of life, you are 'Today's Special.' And tomorrow's. And the day after that. And…well, you get the drift. Yes, that's right. We may be the king, but you, my friend, are the almighty ruler.

Seriously. That's what it said. I have a picture.

It promised me the world, just like TV. I had half a mind to test their extravagant promises by walking up to the counter and asking for my own universe in a bag, or something equally preposterous, like a Big Mac. But I'm sure the stereotypical teenager in my imagination—basically, *Superbad*'s Jonah Hill wearing a BK cap—would reply, "I'm sorry sir, we don't serve Big Macs here. This is not a McDonald's. This is Burger King. We serve Whoppers."

And I would reply, "Well can you put an extra patty on that, and maybe put half of a bun between the patties, and then put special sauce on it? Oh and don't forget the pickles and sesame seeds."

"No, sir, we can't do that. You can order a regular Whopper, Angry Whopper, or Whopper Jr."

"But your sign says I can have it my way."

"That's just rhetoric, sir."

"What's rhetoric?"

"Rhetoric is when you say something you don't mean to get people to like you. Or in our case, buy our greasy food."

"…

…

(//speechlessness)

Well, you are surprisingly articulate for a worker bee on the bottom rung of corporate America. And honest. But don't you think that's like, immoral or something?"

At this point, I'm sure our chubby antagonist would inevitably offer one of the two most hackneyed excuses of all time.

Either,

A: "Everyone else is doing it." A statement subtly underscored by the compulsory shoulder shrug.

Or,

B: "Whatever dude, I just work here." A statement not so subtly underscored by the combined action of rolling the eyes and raising the brow.

Unfortunately, either of these comebacks would effectively disarm my penetrating query with a perfect blend of stupidity, irreverence, and cunning linguistic skills. Damn corporate bureaucracies and their clever drones. I apologize if your first job was at Burger King. Dane Cook.[40]

The BK propaganda wasn't only written on the walls, either. It was written on my cup, too. It read,

---

[40] Another vulgar comedian who often references his first job at Burger King, aka 'the BK lounge.'

This cup makes a statement about you. It says 'Hey, look at me. I'm an ambitious and decisive person.' You could have gone larger, but you didn't. You could have gone smaller, but you decided against it. No, you know exactly what you want in life and that you should always have it *your* way.

Again, I have a picture.

When I took another sip from that cup, a small part of me died. I don't believe that I am an almighty ruler. I don't think that I'm a god. That thought is very frightening to me, because I wouldn't be able to handle the pressure. I would make for a pretty awful god. People like Richard Dawkins would be justified in telling people not to believe in me.

Neither do I think that I am "defined" by my cup. I don't believe that people form opinions on me based on the fact that I am sipping Diet Coke from a medium sized cup at Burger King. Can you imagine it? "Hey, that guy chose a medium cup! He must be *ambitious*. And *decisive*. I wonder if he's sipping *diet* Coke. That means he cares about his health. But he's also hip, and authentic, because Coke is "The Real Thing." I should be friends with *him*."

Dang. If life were like this, I'd be the most popular guy around. But as nice as these marketing gimmicks sound, buying Frosted Flakes or BK burgers will not lead to instant popularity, happiness and success. Still, this is what people who are in charge of selling hamburgers want me to believe: that if I buy their burger, people will like me: that I will be young again: that life will be like it is on TV.

It is a worldview that has been taught to us since birth by the postmodern spectacle of sleaze and excess. And the lazy, self obsessed generation you see before you, Mr. C.K., is the helpless victim: bred into submission by repetitive marketing schemes and clever gimmicks, we have been corrupted, stripped of our pocket change, our innocence, and the ability to enjoy the simpler things in life, all in the name of selling more Frosted Flakes.

5. As we experience disappointment in these colossal promises, we usually react in one of two ways. Either we become like drug addicts, chasing effervescent highs, or we decay into irrepressible cynics, incapable of hope or sincerity. The spiritual condition and emotional fortitude of 'Generation Me'[41] is now ineffably bleak; a result of the emotional propaganda that is, as David Foster Wallace says,

> like somebody who smiles warmly at you only because he wants something from you. This is dishonest, but what's sinister is the cumulative effect that such dishonesty has on us: since it offers a perfect facsimile or simulacrum of goodwill without goodwill's real spirit, it messes with our heads and eventually starts upping our defenses even in cases of genuine smiles and real art and

---

[41] The title of the previously quoted book by sociologist Jean Twenge.

62

true goodwill. It makes us feel confused and lonely and impotent and angry and scared. It causes despair.[42]

Advertising, to the overexposed, causes despair.

Thom Yorke (of Radiohead) says basically the same thing: our emotions have been "stolen to sell products."[43]

When we hear that BK offers love inside a burger, and try it out, and find it to be unsatisfying, we begin to harbor suspicion towards real love. As we learn to protect our hearts from the disappointment of fake love, we lose the ability to experience real love. Either we develop cynical safeguards, or we simply sink into submission to grease-saturated disappointment. In either case, we quickly lose self-confidence, and start to feel bad about ourselves. Which is exactly where the advertisers want us.

People who are dumb and despairing and disillusioned make for the best consumers. They just keep buying, keep trying to fill our emptiness with the latest TV-approved product.

Keeping up with this lifestyle is *exhausting*. Mentally. Physically. And most of all, spiritually. Louis C.K. might call us the crappiest

---

[42] David Foster Wallace, *A Supposedly Fun Thing I'll Never Do Again*, 289

[43] Thom Yorke, when discussing the song *Let Down*: "In the advert, the emotions aren't genuine. But if they were - if there was a camera in front of two people genuinely feeling that way, well, everyone's already seen the car advert, so that genuine emotion has been circumvented forever. There are certain emotions you think are trite, certain things you'd never say to your partner because it's corny. Because it's been stolen to sell products." - Mary Gaitskill, `Radiohead: Alarms and Surprises', Alternative Press, April, 1998.

generation, but I would inject that this is because we are also the most manipulated generation. After all, we have been raised,

> not as a part of the natural world—like the 30,000
> generations before—but in a synthetic reality. A reality
> defined by advertising, media and consumer-driven
> culture… (this generation has) been hyped, suckered,
> aroused, thrilled—their fears, needs and desires ma-
> nipulated in the most grotesque ways. Capitalist hype
> is the music of their anxiety, the gray noise of their de-
> pression, the muzak of their despair.[44]

Somehow, in this spectacle of products and hype, we have lost touch with ourselves. We have grown used to this cage: this "thicket of unreality which stands between us and the facts of life."[45] Like Robin Williams' adult Peter Pan in *Hook*,[46] we have forgotten who we once were.

So how do we change? How do we rescue those innocent elements of our childhood that were suppressed, and discipline those spoiled childish desires that grew out of control? I need a revolution— one which begins as an idea, continues as a feeling, and grows into a lifestyle. I must learn to notice the ways that our world—everything from Oprah to Burger King to Tony the Tiger —has shaped me, and be-

---

[44] Kalle Lasn, creator of Adbusters magazine, from his blog on adbusters.org

[45] Daniel Boorstin. *The Image: A Guide to Pseudo-Events in America*, 3

[46] My favorite childhood film. I thought it needed a shout out.

trayed me: to notice the ways that our world took my innocent heart and infected it with disillusionment, disappointment, and despair. I need to reject the so called "freedom" that is offered every time I flick on the TV or walk down the cereal aisle in the supermarket.

Together, we must learn to pursue what David Foster Wallace calls "real freedom." The freedom that comes from "being educated, and understanding how to think." Otherwise, we may sacrifice ourselves on the altar of economic progress. Our addictions to comfort and excess and Frosted Flakes will steer us towards nothing but **"unconsciousness, the default setting, the rat race, the constant gnawing sense of having had, and lost, some infinite thing."**[47]

Outro:

"People say that your dreams are the only things that save you
C'mon baby, we don't dream
We can live on this behavior
Every time you close your eyes,
lies, lies."

- *Rebellion (Lies)* by The Arcade Fire

---

[47] David Foster Wallace, *This is Water*. Such a good quote, I had to use it twice.

Three.

On High School
Or, *I Mostly Copy Other People*

Recommended listening:

Smells Like Teen Spirit by Nirvana

"Here we are now, entertain us."

Or, this:

I was having burritos with my friend Shad[48] this one time after shooting some hoops at the UBC gym. Somehow, we started talking about *Survivor*, and how it's pretty symbolic of modern life, even if nobody notices. Here's some of what he had to say:

> All I know is I saw one episode and it consisted of adults playing children's games. One game was 'who can stand on a log the longest.' Seriously. That was the whole extent of the game. Even kids are too smart to play that. I felt like punching all of them. At one point one lady was crying because she missed her kids. And I wanted to cry *for* her kids because their mother is INSANE for leaving them for six weeks so she can play Duck-Duck-Goose competitively with other forty-year olds on the slim chance that she might get money from winning a game show that doesn't even make sense. All around, worst show possible and all the more enraging that so many people watched it. Shame on all of us.

He's right. *Survivor* doesn't really make sense: unless you view it as a satire of modern life. Because after all, what *is* life if not a game of competitive Duck-Duck Goose for money and fame, right? From this

---

[48] He raps for a living. Check out his rhymes on YouTube: "Biggest thing outta Canada since Pamela's double D's." Nice, right?

perspective, *Survivor* portrays the… what's the word… *ri-DIC-ulousness* of our everyday lives transposed to the stage of a deserted island. Here, we can watch and laugh at people who basically live the same lives that we do, only on a much smaller scale, in a much different environment. People do what they have to in order to "survive." But surviving isn't just about surviving the elements. Mostly, it's about surviving other people: maintaining one's spot in the tribe, and then convincing people to vote for you in the end. Basically, you win by achieving popularity.

The real tragedy is that *Survivor* isn't meant to be ironic. If it was intended to be a sarcastic take on modern life, we should call it art, and put a few seasons on display in a museum for future generations to appreciate. However, I don't think the show's creator, Mark Burnett, is trying to present a wince-inducing caricature of modern life. He's just trying to make money and entertain people. He's just trying to play the game, too: the game of life, where you *also* win by getting popular.

The phenomenon of *Survivor*, I think, is a pretty good metaphor for the environment and patterns of our daily lives. We watch the show on TV, and it looks like fun. You see a number of different ways to play the game—different roles and strategies. Many of us want to give it a try: to sign up to go to the island, and play by their rules, with hopes and dreams of winning the game and becoming rich and famous for emasculating ourselves on national television.

What we don't realize, however, is that the game changes you. I imagine that if you actually got to play *Survivor*, you'd quickly realize that they didn't show you everything on TV: the hardships, the confusion, the despair. Playing the game is a lot harder in real life. Still, you'd plug along, hoping that in the end it will all be worthwhile. But even if

68

you won, when you returned home, you'd find that you've lost a part of yourself. Maybe your character has been corrupted. Maybe you've lost some dignity. Maybe, outside of the game, you're not sure who you are anymore. So you just want to try again. You just want to keep playing.

When Survivor first came on, I remember thinking to myself, "Man, I wish I could be on that show. I bet I could win, and still find a way to be honest, and not make a fool of myself. Do they let fifteen year olds go on *Survivor*? They should make one for teenagers."

Which, of course, they already have. It's called high school— and it's been on TV for much longer than *Survivor*.

-

Until age twelve, I grew up without a television in my house. Still, I occasionally found ways to inject some exciting cartoon action into my dreary afternoons with the likes of *Batman*, *Spiderman*, *Darkwing Duck* and *Captain Planet*. I watched them at friend's houses, at the neighbors, at Grandma's: *anywhere* to get my fix. But the one show I was really into was *Ninja Turtles*—which, technically, I wasn't "allowed" to watch, because of all the violence and subtle Buddhism.

I remember feeling angry with my parents for forbidding me to watch *Ninja Turtles*. There wasn't any real danger in watching that show, I thought, because even *I* understand that a cartoon about talking, fighting, mutant *turtles*[49] is not realistic, and should not be imitated. Also, I didn't pay any attention to Splinter's religious persuasion, because Splinter wasn't

---

[49] MOM. They're TURTLES. *I can't watch a show about turtles? TURTLES???* ARE YOU SERIOUS? Mom. They're turtles, mom. Come. *On.*

cool like Michelangelo, who was too busy eating pizza and making wise-cracks to be meditating.

I'll tell you the show that I should not, under any circumstances, have been allowed to watch.

Saved by the Bell.

Why? Because I *did* try to imitate this show, which made unrealistic expectations of life seem realistic. It taught me what was important about growing up: to live a life that looks and feels just like *Saved by the Bell*. Just like *Survivor*, I watched carefully, and learned the roles and strategies. And I desperately wanted to give it a try: to play the game for myself.

As our friend Chuck Klosterman says, "Understanding *Saved by the Bell* meant you understood what was supposed to define the ultra-simplistic, hyperstereotypical high school experience—and understanding that formula meant you realized **what was important about growing up**…. *Saved by the Bell* wasn't real, but neither is most of reality.[50]"

Chuck is basically saying three things:

(1)   There is a cultural template of what high school should look like, based upon shows like *Saved by the Bell*, which is followed (more or less) by most high school students in North America.

(2)   Having the right experiences in high school is equivalent to growing up. Again, you have the experience first, and perhaps learn a few lessons along the way. If you must.

---

[50] From *Sex, Drugs and Cocoa Puffs*. Again. Emphasis mine.

(3)   Because so many people try to live out a fantastic delusion of what high school should look like, the very fabric of our reality has been changed—meaning, many people never stop playing by the rules of high school. Including, on more days than I'd like to admit, myself.

The propaganda of *Saved by the Bell, Degrassi, The OC* and a glut of high school themed 80's movies shaped the present reality in which I live, breathe, and shop. They taught me that life, during those awkward teenage years, was a game to be played, like *Survivor*. Even though I finished high school, I never felt like I won the game: so I still have a thirst to keep playing. And I'm beginning to see that if I'm going to find any *real* meaning in life, outside of this soul-crushing disgrace of a Duck-Duck-Goose game, I have to learn to see if for what it is: a hoax cooked up by Nike, NBC and Hollywood to get us to buy more stuff and watch more television.

Before watching *Saved by the Bell*, most of the shows I loved featured heroes of some sort. This was useful, I guess, because finding a good hero is an essential part of one's education. It helps informs our aspirations by providing a (more or less) tangible ideal. When I was growing up, I had the same heroes as most other kids. Batman and Spiderman taught me that there were some evil people in the world that needed to be stopped, but most other people are decent, and occasionally need to be saved. Hence, lots of us kids wanted to be firemen or policemen, so we could fight the bad guys, and help the people who needed helping. That way, we could wear costumes, and be like our heroes, if only just a little.

I'd say this is actually a pretty decent goal for one's life: to become someone who knows and cares about justice: someone who is willing to sacrifice for the greater good. But along the way, something changed.

Somewhere between the ages of eight and sixteen, our dreams 'evolved.' And instead of saving the world, we began to dream of something much less important. We dreamed of one day becoming *cool*.

I think I can trace the moment that my dreams changed back to a time when I decided I could never grow up to be like Batman. On that day, I changed heroes—and the entire course of my life changed. Around the time I turned nine years old, I took on a new hero. This hero—the person I aspired to be like more than anyone—didn't have big muscles. He didn't fight crime, or tame wild beasts, or fight evil robots with num-chucks. Instead, my hero was *cool*.

Yes, I will admit it. Zach Morris, that paradigm unto himself of high-school themed sitcoms, became *my hero*. My life would never be the same. Zach was the character whose crazy antics and clever comebacks sucked us into the world of high school, Bayside style, in *Saved by the Bell,* the most popular Saturday morning sitcom of the early nineties. He was always getting into trouble, with girls, bullies, the principal, you name it; but he always found a clever way of escaping the usual consequences. Things always had a way of working out for him.

Zach was successful at *everything*. He was good-looking, funny, popular, and dated a cheerleader. He was also musical. He sang in the glee club, and had his own band, called *The Zach Attack*. On top of this, Zach could freeze time simply by saying "Time out!" while making a 'T' sign with his hands. Call it pizzazz, panache or whatever; Zach had it all in spades. Is there anyone in the history of the planet who was cooler than this guy? I didn't think so.

However, it wasn't long before I entered high school and discovered that the success enjoyed by Mr. Popular didn't come easily. In fact, I couldn't figure out how he did it. Perhaps I should have clued into the fact that *Saved by the Bell* isn't real, and all of Zach's lines were scripted. But hey, I was, like, twelve. (High school actually starts in middle school). I really believed that Bayside reflected an authentic high school experience. I didn't clue into the fact that the show wasn't supposed to be taken seriously. Twelve-year-olds take *everything* seriously.[51]

My expectations of high school left me high and dry. Although the roles remained (largely) the same, in the real world, nobody tells you what to do or what to say, there aren't any studio audiences to appease your unfunny remarks with canned laughter, and things do not always work out for the best. In the 'real world' of high school, I found that panache was out, and sarcasm was in. Also, people swore a lot, they had 'pre-marital' sex, and they listened to Eminem, who is basically the Bizarro-world version of the Fresh Prince (another important high school icon). And you know what? I had a hard time adjusting, because apparently it's *not* cool to be friends with nerds and play the Keytar wearing zigzag decorated suspenders while lip-syncing to James Brown at the eighth grade talent show. In other words, it's *not* cool to be just like Zach Morris. At least, not anymore.

Sure, Zach was popular, and gaining popularity is also the goal of the high school good life. But this process is much more complicated in real life: especially if you don't look like Mr. Morris. For the rest of us, high school is dictated by all sorts of complicated social norms. For

---

[51] At least, twelve year olds in the 90's. They didn't understand sarcasm like today's twelve year olds.

instance, you can't be friends with people like Screech in real high school. Also, God help you if you wrestle.

High school enforced a strange set of rules on the fresh faced, naïve dreamer I was at age twelve. It forced me to absorb a predetermined identity—a disguise—just to get by. I had to choose friends that helped me climb the social ladder. I had to wear the right clothes, and listen to the right music. I had to watch closely what I said, and what I did, because slip-ups can haunt you forever. I had to play the game, like *Survivor*: to achieve enough popularity points to stay on with the tribe.

The game of high school serves as a training ground for a world where appearances matter more than character, relationships are made for the sake of networking, knowledge is gained simply to pass a test or impress a boss, and getting by is more important than changing things. Understand these rules, and you might just win. High school is basically a training ground for the *Survivor*-esque game we call "the real world."[52]

This was the path I was led down by my hero. I wanted to be like him, to live like he did, to experience what I'd seen on TV *so much* that I gave up a part of myself along the way. But now that I think about it, in what kind of world is Zach Morris somebody's hero? When I think of a prototypical hero, I think of someone big and tough and courageous. I

---

[52] John Mayer was wrong (in *No Such Thing*). Unless you happen to *be* John Mayer, who, conspicuously, has managed to break the rules of the actual real world, being an average looking dude who has dated famous 90's Jennifers Aniston and Love Hewitt, not to mention Jessica Simpson. I can't even *imagine* what Karma has in store for him. If I believed in Karma.

think of someone who deserves glory and respect, someone who defends the helpless, who inspires virtue, and probably carries around a sword. Zach Morris, on the other hand, just washed his hair a lot.

I'm sure if you were to study the history of hero figures, you'd find that heroes were legendary characters described by the poets as the kinds of people crucially needed in society. Back in the day, society needed strong workers, courageous leaders, and fearless fighters. So you had stories about guys like Robin Hood, Achilles, Beowulf, and King Arthur. Now those guys were *heroes*. But what does society need today?

Society needs people who are easily convinced to buy useless crap. It needs people who want to be cool like Zach Morris—people willing to do and buy *anything* to achieve this status. There is something wrong when people start idolizing people like Zach and Kelly.[53] Those characters were basically just advertising gimmicks, "role models" cooked up by corporate marketing executives who needed to sell more Nikes. By offering up "heroes" like Zach, a high school pseudogod, they brainwashed us. They convinced us that life was not about imitating Batman, and trying to save people, but rather, that it is about imitating Zach, who had mastered the art of looking cool. In so doing, they helped turn high school into a cultural phenomenon that initiates the young and impressionable into the dominant lifestyle of North American culture—consumerism—by promising the one thing we've been taught by to crave more than anything: popularity.

---

[53] Zach's girlfriend, the head cheerleader.

"High school is a North American obsession," Douglas Coupland says.[54] Most other countries don't have proms, cheerleaders, high school football, pep rallies, school plays, or even air-band Fridays in the cafeteria. It's true. High school just isn't that big of a deal in the rest of the world.

In North America, however, it is a world of insatiable fascination. Here, the winning Quarterback or head Cheerleader can live like a celebrity. They can be named King or Queen on prom-night, cementing their celebrity status with *actual crowns*. Nobody rewards mediocrity quite like we do.

So how did the stage of high school, those four years of awkward maturation, become such a cultural phenomenon? Was it all Zach's fault? No. There were a million teen idols like Zach. And a million shows—and movies—like *Saved by the Bell*.

During the 1980's, America shone a spotlight on the world of high school and discovered a new genre: the coming-of-age story. If you check out a list of the top fifty high-school themed movies of all time, more than half were made in the 80's. It's like, all of a sudden, they decided the rest of life wasn't interesting enough, and angst-y teenage dramedies[55] became all the rage. The world of high school became like a stage, something that everyone who grew up watching these shows and films wanted to experience on their own. By ingesting these films, we were exposed to the sorts of things that usually happen at this time, and high school became more than just a means to an education: it became a

---

[54] In *JPod*

[55] Dramatic Comedies.

checklist of must-have experiences. Through the propaganda of 1980's Hollywood, a set of regimented ideas and behaviors became cemented as the typical high school experience.

Don't believe me? Preposterous, you say? Go watch the 2010 film *Easy A,* where Emma Page's character Olive, the central figure in another high school sex comedy, expresses the deepest desires of her heart:

> I want John Cusack holding a boombox outside my window.[56] I want to ride off on a lawnmower with Patrick Dempsey.[57] I want Jake from *Sixteen Candles* waiting outside the church for me. I want Judd Nelson thrusting his fist into the air because he knows he got me.[58] *Just once I want my life to be like an 80's movie.*

To Olive, high school is a place where she is supposed to find love, because this is what she was taught by Hollywood. Let's take a closer look at some of these films, to see what other desires have been drilled into our psyches.

Exhibit #1: *The Breakfast Club*
Director: John Hughes
Popular Actors:

---

[56] from *Say Anything*
[57] from *Can't Buy Me Love*
[58] from *The Breakfast Club*

Emilio Estevez (pre-*Mighty Ducks*)

Molly Ringwald (80's high school movie starlet.)

Ally Sheedy (also very big in the 80s)

On that *Top 50* list I mentioned, this film sits on top. Here, five seniors that happen to represent different social cliques spend a Saturday in detention together. They are asked to write an essay on "who you think you are." The movie begins with their answer:

> Dear Mr. Vernon, we accept the fact that we had to sacrifice a whole Saturday in detention for whatever it was that we did wrong. What we did *was* wrong. But we think you're crazy to make us write this essay telling you who we think we are. What do you care? You see us as you want to see us... in the simplest terms and the most convenient definitions. You see us as a brain, an athlete, a basket case, a princess and a criminal. Correct? That's the way we saw each other at seven o'clock this morning. We were brainwashed.

Since these kids were forced to spend their entire Saturday together, they managed to find some common ground to help transcend their social differences. They discussed problems with parents, anxieties about growing up, dealing with the awkwardness of being sixteen and other sob stories drenched in teen-angst. By the end, however, they resign themselves to the cruelties of the system, to the fact that high school is far too political a world for relationships to rise above social distinction, and they go back to playing their various roles in their so called "reality."

Best quote:

Allison Reynolds: "When you grow up, your heart dies."

Message about High School:

-     The system rules. You are given a particular identity associated with your social class but which also factors in your talent, grades and looks, and this identity will determine your life. You will always be judged based on a set of criteria pre-determined by popular culture. There is no escape.

-     When you grow up, you will get a job and live a boring life, so you might as well live it up while you're young.

-     At some high schools, there is such a thing as a Physics Club.

Exhibit #2: *Can't Buy Me Love.*

Director: Steve Rash

Popular Actor: Patrick Dempsey (of *Grey's Anatomy*)

You may have never even heard of this movie (even though Olive quotes it), but it's one of my personal favorites. It's about a nerdy kid with the unfortunate luck to have been named Ronald. He bribes his neighbor, Cindi Mansini, the most popular girl in school, to date him for a month, so that he can discover what it's like to be cool. He eventually accomplishes his goal, but learns that real friendships are more important than climbing the social ladder.

Best quotes:

-      Ronald's friend: "They've all become your disciples. I've seen zombies with more individuality."

-      Ronald Miller: "We do have a lot of great memories but be honest... wouldn't you like to be popular?"

Kenneth Wurman: "And have to be in a clique? No."

-      Ronald Miller: What happened to us? We were all friends in elementary.

Kenneth Wurman: "That's because we were all forced to be in the same room together. But, hey, Junior high, high school? Forget it. Jocks became Jocks. Cheerleaders became cheerleaders. We became us."

Message about High School:

-      The end goal is popularity: being cool. Social acceptance equals happiness. This is based almost entirely upon image, which can easily be manipulated, and destroyed.

-      Once you leave the confines of elementary for a large school, you end up spending most of your time with people who are like you, people who will constantly reinforce your chosen identity and habits.

Exhibit #3: *Rebel Without A Cause.*

Director: Nicholas Ray

Popular Actor: James Dean

Now, *Rebel Without A Cause* is actually from the 50's. But it laid the foundation for every film about the competitive, spiritually-suffocating world of high school to come. It also introduced us to the late James Dean, a young man immortalized as the "coolest" to have ever graced the screen, a legacy cemented by the fact that he died young, pretty much the coolest thing you can do.

The story follows Jim Stark, played by Dean, on his first day at school in a new town. Knife-fights, "Chicken Runs"[59] and endless cigarette smoking ensue. More importantly however, the aesthetic of "cool" is born, typified by the film's aloof, composed, charming and defiant protagonist. The "rebel without a cause," "live-fast, die-young" lifestyle becomes a template for "cool" that informs the fantasies of teens everywhere. It is also quickly hijacked by advertising agencies that push cigarettes, fast cars, and leather jackets.

Best Quotes:
- Jim Stark (to parents): You're tearing me apart!
- Jim Stark: If I had one day when I didn't have to be all confused and I didn't have to feel that I was ashamed of everything. If I felt that I belonged someplace, you know?

(James was not only the template of cool, but also, I suppose, of teen angst. Thus begins the cinema's long and tumultuous history with angst-y characters. Thank you, James. Without you, I suppose I would

---

[59] Where you drive towards a cliff and the last one to hit the brake wins. Another fun game I'd like to try.

have been deprived the joys of the wall-piercing cries of countless college roommates trying to play *Hands Down* by Dashboard Confessional at three in the morning.)[60]

Message about High School:

- The coolest kid at school is usually the rebel, and is his own authority figure. Instead of conforming to others, others conform to him.

- True individuality is rebellion. And rebellion is having the right jacket, car, and hairstyle. A cigarette in one hand; a match in the other.

- If you want girls to like you, be really angst-y. (However, in my experience, this only works if you also happen to be really good looking.)

These films and countless others offered us a template, or script. There are different roles you can take on, like the jock, the rebel, the cheerleader, or the brain. These roles come attached to certain gangs or cliques, which enforce the rules and stereotypes ruthlessly. It also offers situations you can play out, like confrontations with teachers, or parents, but mostly with other groups of students who represent different social classes or lifestyle choices.[61]

The world of high school, made up by students trying desperately to enact their ideal high school experience, becomes like a stage: a place where *you too* can win the big game, date the perfect girl, or get the lead in the play. Where *you too* can be the centre of attention. While

---

[60] That's an inside joke for people familiar with the term 'emo.'

[61] The best example being when two groups that are pretty much the exact same try to kill each other, like in *West Side Story,* or *Bring it On.*

in theory, this may seem exciting, in reality, the pressure that we feel to live up to these expectations spurs endless anxiety. And this anxiety changes you. Through desperation to get good grades, please your parents, date the girl or make the team—to live out our Hollywood-inspired, *Survivor*-esque expectations of what our young lives should be like—we find ourselves giving into the belief that this game is real. Sometimes we need to be reminded that there are other ways to play, and worlds outside of this game. We need other ways of understanding and dealing with anxiety.

I could try to argue for a change in the way we choose to educate our adolescents, but I'd rather let Hollywood do it for me. There is one 80's film that radically breaks from the typical John Hughes mold. It's called *Dead Poets Society*. It stars Robin Williams, Ethan Hawke, and the other doctor from *House*.

This film shows the pressures facing teens in high school with greater emotional depth and clarity than any other I've seen. It explores the stresses that develop from high expectations to succeed, levied heavily by parents and teachers; the coercive force of parents that make us choose particular classes or extra-curriculars; the tension between living in the moment—seizing the day—and preparing for the future; and finally, the desire to refrain from getting into trouble versus the desire to really live.

Being young is tough. This film chooses not to reduce these stresses to parodies of sexual frustration, of nerdy stereotypes grasping helplessly at the straws of popularity. Instead, it paints a portrait of youth in its complexity, reflecting upon both its tragedy and brevity. In other words, go rent it.

Robin Williams plays John Keating, a new teacher at Welton Academy, one of the most renowned all-boys schools in the country. His approach to education stands in stark contrast to the boys' other teachers. For instance, on the first day of school, he asks them to rip out certain pages from their books, and later, to stand on their desks.

"Why do I stand upon my desk? I stand here to remind myself that we must constantly look at things in a different way," he says.

It's a good lesson.

He also teaches them to read poetry. *Sl-ow-ly*. With emphasis. With emotion and empathy, rather than scientific logic. To him, poetry is an expression of the human condition, and it cannot be reduced to formula's and equations. It cannot be quantified or understood by method. Like life itself, it can only be breathed, and lived.

The kind of education he offers is radically opposed to that which is offered by the rest of the school. His colleagues openly admit to seeking conformity and control over the students through the board approved curriculum and structure. When Keating queries the headmaster, declaring "I always thought the idea of education was to think for yourself," the headmaster replies, "At these boys' age? Not on your life." Keating believes that a real education does not suppress the human spirit because it is volatile, dangerous, and difficult to harness. A real education, like the one he offers, helps to channel the human spirit towards its greatest potential in expression, ingenuity, and courageous thought.

What's more, Keating recognizes the dangers of conformity— "the difficulty of maintaining your own beliefs in the face of others"— and warns his students against these dangers: "We all have a great need for acceptance. But you must trust that your beliefs are unique, your own, even though others may think them odd, or unpopular, even though the Herd may go (summoning Robin Williams-esque cartoony sheep voice,) 'that's baaa-aa-aad.'"

You must *own* your beliefs. Unfortunately, high school is often a hindrance, rather than a help, to the activity of taking ownership. Instead of learning to stand against the tides like a post, planted in something solid, we learn to merely drift on the whimsical cultural tides of popular sentiment, driven by a craving for acceptance that drowns out desire for true wisdom and knowledge.

Like Mr. Keating, I think that we must come to a place where we hold values and beliefs because they seem good and true, not because they help us obtain popularity, or the system's idea of success.[62]

The people at Nike and NBC don't care about us. Trying to play the game they've set out for us is a waste of time. The first step towards growing up, and getting a real education, is realizing that the person that you and I were in high school is not real. There's so much more to an identity than a fashion and a clique, and so much more to life than a checklist of experiences.

Many people, unfortunately, never figure this out. Instead, they live their lives totally oblivious to what high school has become, and the conditioning it offers us: the script, the roles, the subconscious checklist of experiences. They don't come to realize that the cultural phenomenon of high school is largely a scheme to get people like me to accept certain

---

[62] This is pretty much the underlying theme for the whole book, by the way. Just thought I'd let you know, in case you missed it amongst all the razz-matazz pop culture references.

ideas and structures that aren't realistic; a plan to indoctrinate us with the rules and rhythms of consumer society, where popularity, success and love can be bought and sold. It's all a hoax: one that convinced me to give up on my childhood dreams of changing the world: one that infected my ability to have wholesome relationships and colored my self-worth in terms that are entirely dependent upon the flimsy acceptance of my peers.

In short, I, too, was brainwashed.

At least, that's what they called it in *The Breakfast Club*. Perhaps this is a suitable description. Dictionary.com says that brainwashing is,

1   A forcible indoctrination to induce someone to give up basic political, social, or religious beliefs and attitudes and to accept contrasting regimented ideas.

2   Persuasion by propaganda or salesmanship.

Depending on where you went to high school, you may draw the line between "forcible indoctrination" and "persuasion by propaganda" differently, but no doubt you'll agree that something like brainwashing goes on. It began when we were kids and our mom's took us to matinees of *Back to the Future*, or when we dug into our brothers' collection to find a copy of *Risky Business*. It started with the "propaganda" of 80's high school movies, and continued with TV shows like *Saved by the Bell,* which convinced us to buy into the spirit killing world of high school, simply because it looked like fun at the time. We became used to the idea that this is what is, and this is what should be, and we, like the

members of *The Breakfast Club,* resigned ourselves to helpless surrender: You can't really blame us, Mr. Vernon…

    We just wanted to play the game.

Four.

On Video Games
Or, *You Can't Play* The Sims *Forever*

Recommended Listening:

Requiem for a Dream: *Two Towers Remix* by Clint Mansell—basically
the most epic song ever.

Or the theme song to Tetris.

"In the morning I walked to the bank. I went to the automated
teller machine to check my balance. I inserted my card, entered my secret code, tapped out my request. The figure on the screen roughly
corresponded to my independent estimate, feebly arrived at after long
searches through documents, tormented arithmetic. Waves of relief and
gratitude flowed over me. The system had blessed my life. I felt its sup-

port and approval. The system hardware, the mainframe sitting in the locked room in some distant city. What a pleasing interaction. I sensed that something of deep personal value, but not money, not that at all, had been authenticated and confirmed. A deranged person was escorted from the bank by two armed guards. The system was invisible, which made it all the more impressive, all the more disquieting to deal with. But we were in accord, at least for now. The networks, the circuits, the streams, the harmonies."

   —   Don DeLillo, *White Noise*

"The Matrix has you."

    - *The Matrix*

1. The sun ascends slowly over the plains of Azeroth, and I, a

lowly level-six Night Elf, stand perched on a hill—acquiescent—calmly anticipating the challenges of a new day. The daunting task of killing the formidable Hogger lies before me—just another foe to best on the road towards becoming champion of the Alliance. From a distance I spot my opponent… survey the field of battle… let out a Commanding Shout, and charge! Let the panoramic carnage begin!

    Sigh. A part of me curses the fact that I don't live in Middle Earth. Life just isn't very exciting in this synthetic eco-system we have erected to protect ourselves from the dark, dangerous world we once knew. Let's face it: many of us retreat to the virtual world of fantasy because life as *we* know it is *boring.* As evidenced by the popularity of stories like *Harry Potter* and *Lord of the Rings,* I'm not alone in my desire for something more, something mysterious, something… magical. It's a romantic thought to believe there is a time and place where such things as wizards and dragons and elves exist. A world like this would be so exciting… so dangerous… so AWESOME. Even though I can't visit a place like this, somebody out there knows I want to, and helped to create the next best thing: an MMORPG[63] called *World of Warcraft*.

In this game you start by choosing to be an elf character or a dwarf or whatever, and you learn the ropes by going on adventures to get better swords and armor and the like. You get potions to heal your-self, make friends to help you on your missions, and develop your skills to deal with new challenges. If you don't have time to sign up, you can watch the South Park episode about it, which offers a good summary.

Some people spend *hours and hours* on end in *WoW* carrying out well-laid plans to develop their character by vanquishing enemies and obtaining treasures. "Kill, get treasure, repeat."[64] Here, there is a new mission for every new day. The possibilities are endless.

In *WoW*, there is such a thing as a quest. This is the whole point of the game, really: to go on quests. You start with pretty simple ones that don't take much experience or skill, and then build your character and find teammates to help you move on. I bemoan the fact that in my life, the closest thing I can think of that would be deemed a 'quest' is saving enough money to buy a new iPhone.

---

[63] Massively Multiplayer Online Role Playing Game. But I bet you already knew that, didn't you.

[64] A line borrowed from Benjamin Barber in *Consumed*.

This world provides near complete escape from real life. There, the suffocating pressures of our own reality can be forgotten. In real life, you might work for a guy named Michael Scott at Dunder/Mifflin Paper Co, drive a green '03 Accord and spend every Tuesday night at Applebee's. But in the *World of Warcraft*, you can be a feared hunter, marry an elf princess, fight with a clan and ride a tiger.

!

As well, in this game you are not judged by your looks, or car, or pants, but solely by your ability to battle orcs.[65]

For many of us, this world is more attractive than our own. It speaks to our desires for adventure, romance, mystery, and magic, without insisting that we leave the basement. It makes the purest, most satisfying highs of life easily accessible to anyone with a PC and a LAN connection.

The 36-year-old guy with a pony tail who plays *WoW* religiously in his mom's basement may be a laughable stereotype, but I would argue that there's a little of that guy in all of us. To one degree or another, we all prefer virtual reality to our own.

And why not?

Real life is confusing. It's messy. It's disappointing. In real life, adventure takes money and effort and planning and danger.[66] However, real danger does not mix well with my addiction to air conditioning, Frappuccinos, and general protection from the elements, so I've become used to living vicariously through people like Indiana Jones and Master

---

[65] By clicking a mouse really, really fast.

[66] For instance, it costs about a hundred grand and a year of training to climb Everest.

Chief. That's why they made *World of Warcraft*, for people like me, who want the thrills of life as a Warrior Elf while maintaining access to a fridge full of cola and microwaveable burritos.

Post-modern life at its finest.

In real life, our world is also complicated. There are problems that don't have easy solutions. In the game, however, life is simple. First, you choose a side: either good or evil. There's no moral grey area when it comes to doing battle, no such thing as an existential crisis. Second, you don't sit around wondering how to pass the time while you wait to die. You go on a mission. There are various missions you can choose from, with direct objectives and tangible rewards. You spend time developing your character/avatar so you can take on larger missions. I think that the simplicity of this life, of this way of being, appeals to many people who may get bogged down in the overwhelming complexity of "RL" (gamer lingo for "real life"), and its mind-numbing monotony. Plus, there's no re-spawn in RL.[67]

Unless you're Hindu.

Finally, our real world feels *boring*. It's like scientists have figured everything out, so there aren't really any mysteries left. They have decided that there are no such things as ghosts, or demons, or dragons. They have decided that God probably does not exist, and if he does, it's your choice whether you want to follow his rules. As well, they have developed technologies to help us do everything once deemed impossi-

---

[67] Re-spawn refers to starting over when you die in a game. In life, you don't start over when you die. At least, it's still inconclusive. And this is a line from a popular YouTube video, I think.

ble, like getting from one side of the world to another, talking to a friend in Japan, or fighting apocalyptic zombies with a shotgun.

This is how we deal with our boredom. We play games. We make up worlds, whether virtual, political or social, which are easier to understand and find meaning. These worlds come with rules and methods and rewards. Video games are not unique: they are a shining symbol of post-modern life, where you can choose your world, choose your game, and choose your character.

It wasn't always this way. There was a time when you were thrust into a world with established rules and rewards without your permission. You didn't get to choose. In fact, this time looked considerably more like *World of Warcraft* and *LOTR* than ours. It was a time when reality was infused with transcendence and enchantment, a time when people believed in such things as magic and demons and miracles and quests.

Nowadays we tend to call those times "backward" or "ignorant," because people hadn't discovered science yet. But maybe our longing to live in a spiritually infused world, where magic and mystery exist, where science hasn't figured everything out and told us what is and isn't possible, isn't a bad thing. Maybe there is something within us that desires adventure and mystery because deep down we know that life, itself, is a sort of game: with rules, and quests, and rewards. We've just forgotten how to play.

When we stopped believing in magic, in forces of good and evil and the spiritual firmament of life, life itself lost much of its meaning. But when a culture loses touch with a religious worldview, there are consequences. For instance, without God, it's hard to establish any kind of rules. In a game without rules, people get confused, and no one has any fun.

Imagine if there were no rules in *WoW*. People would go online to socialize, and take tours of the forests, but eventually everyone would stop playing because a game without missions and rules is boring and you might as well do something else. Without God, a being who decides the rules of life[68] like Blizzard (the makers of *WoW*) does, we begin to forget whether or not life *itself* has any rules. While some call this "freedom," most of us just get confused, and then bored, because we prefer to play games with rules; so we go play video games instead.

As a culture, for a while, we believed we were on a quest of "progress." This progress basically meant that science and technology emptied our world of spiritual significance for the sake of better healthcare, agriculture, and so on. During the "progress" of our civiliza-tion, we gradually stopped believing that angels and demons existed, and also that life is sort of a big game. Along the way, the meaning of life changed as well. In order to build a society that works, leaders start-ed treating people differently than they did in the Middle Ages. Rather than seeing people as souls to be saved, or barbarians to be civilized, people became things to be controlled. This process was called "mod-ernization." A leading sociologist named Peter Berger explains it pretty well, arguing that:

---

[68] Like morality… just thinking, without the Bible, what would we make our oaths on? Would we even make oaths anymore? Would courtroom proceedings even continue to work, if there was no supernatural threat to tell the truth? Just a thought.

> The transformation of the world brought about by
> the technological innovations of the last few centuries,
> first in Europe and then with increasing rapidity all
> over the world... has had economic, social, and politi-
> cal dimensions, all immense in scope. It has also
> brought on a revolution on the level of human con-
> sciousness, fundamentally uprooting beliefs, values,
> and even the emotional texture of life.[69]

Think about that last line for a second. Through "technological innovation," human consciousness has changed. *We* have changed. We used to go on quests to find meaning. For those of us that still want to go on adventurous quests nowadays, we play video games. Real life is no longer a place for quests, because there are no given rules.

So while this process means it is easier to fly to Maui, or cook dinner, it also means that it's harder to figure out what it means to be human, because the old rules and regulations that guided our under-standing aren't relevant anymore. If you want to find meaning, don't read a book, or ask a priest, or climb a mountain: play a game. Distract yourself.

However, as a whole society commits itself to distraction, we've developed a general sense of hopelessness towards visions of figuring it all out and making peace: of finding an end to our "progress." Maybe this is because we realized the daunting impossibility of this task, or maybe we just got lazy and stopped caring, hoping science and technol-

---

[69] Peter Berger, "Toward a Critique of Modernity," in *Facing Up to Modernity*, 70-1.

ogy would finish the task for us: hoping together they'll build a system which will provide for us, and give us peace, and offer us distraction. Truly, as Allan Bloom said with a faintly discernible despair in his tone, "The end for which (we) had labored for so long has turned out to be amusement."[70] And this is exactly what our culture's brainchildren have accomplished: a system that provides health, wealth, and distraction— at a price.

2. If *WoW* is the best virtual reflection of our past spirit-filled world, *The Sims* is perhaps the best reflection of our current, consumer-driven, relativistic world, because *The Sims* is a game without rules. It is like life, in that there's really no point to the game: you just play. As Chuck Klosterman says, "*The Sims* makes the unconscious conscious, but not in an existential Zen way; *The Sims* forces you to think about how even free people are eternally enslaved by the process of living."[71]

I'm not sure if the makers of *The Sims* meant their creation to be a counter-cultural gaming experience, but as we peer into the mundane, slogging tempo of a life that mimic's our own everyday existence, the meaninglessness of consumerism becomes apparent, as the point of the game seems to be the same as the point of our modern lives: amuse yourself. You ask the same questions about life in *Sim*-world as you do

---

[70] Allan Bloom, *Closing of the American Mind*

[71] CK, *Sex, Drugs, and Cocoa Puffs*

in *this* world, and are then confronted with the painful frustration that it appears there are no answers in *Sim*-world, either.

In this game, you experience life in the most humdrum fashion. You create a character for yourself and set out to get rich and buy lots of stuff. You get friends, impress them with your stuff, and then buy new stuff to replace your old stuff. It even has virtual reality goggles so my *Sim* character can also enjoy computer-mediated escapism. I suppose it's not that exciting being a *Sim*, either. Maybe he'd rather play *WoW* too.

This game is sort of similar to *WoW*, as it features some similar goals: get stuff, and make friends. I'm not sure if you're supposed to kill any demonic beasts though. Maybe I haven't gotten to that level yet. Anyways, on the surface, *The Sims* doesn't have all the stimulating excitement and mystery of *WoW*. *The Sims* features almost no imagination stimulation whatsoever. Perhaps they should introduce fire-breathing monsters—however, my Sim is petulant. He would get scared and run away from a Balroq, or maybe try to tickle it. He wouldn't know what to do—just like me.

So why do people play this game? I'm not entirely sure. I don't really like to play games you can't beat, so I didn't last very long in *Sim* world. In *The Sims*, there is no well-defined goal to your life, like, whoever builds the best mansion wins, or if you get three supermodels to sleep with you, then you beat the game. Like life, there is no score. There are no levels. You just play. I guess the game is probably just about finding happiness, and unfortunately, this isn't any easier a feat in their world than in ours. In *The Sims*, you may spend your time building a vast empire of Penguin Habitats, or talking to a lamp. Nobody can tell you which morality should steer your Sim's life. You just live. And since there's no clear guidelines on what to do, you just kind of wander around doing whatever comes to mind, trying to regulate showers and bathroom breaks and meals, keeping up an appearance of cleanliness, getting to work on time, indulging in the occasional conversation or distraction, and then you die.

This is actually a pretty good description of what it is like to live in the system we have built for ourselves. For the most part, we wander around doing the first few things that come to mind until one day, it's over: "You try to make ends meet, you're a slave to money, then you die."[72] This is our default mode. Like *The Sims,* the game we play doesn't have a score. We used to think, in medieval times, and even into modernity, that there was a "score" to achieve in the game of life. You build an empire. You find salvation. You fight a battle. You marry a princess. You die for your country. You hold chivalrous action in high esteem in the hopes of obtaining honor and glory.

This is how you beat the game. Kind of like in *WoW*.

Nowadays, we aren't so sure there's meaning to life at all. People try to intellectualize this. They try making it sound "existential" and "romantic," like "life is a beautiful, blank canvas waiting for your own unique brushstrokes." But really, it's just boring. We *could* buy into the prevailing notions of success by striving to become actors and rock stars and investment bankers. But why? Would this help us beat the game? Or we could just choose to live life in a completely original, though some might say depressing, way. You might make a conversation partner out

---

72 The Verve, *Bittersweet Symphony*

of a shrubbery, for instance.[73] The prevailing notion today is that the meaning of life is arbitrary. There are no answers. There is no end. The only really relevant question to us entertainment and air conditioning addicts is the same as my *Sim*: how do I avoid boredom?

Many people live lives like they're playing *The Sims*. They ask simple questions that don't have very simple answers, so we get frustrated, and decide to garden instead. And like the computer-simulated versions of ourselves, we float with the tides of popular sentiment. We drift. Instead of digging deeper into the issue, we politely assent to the system's opinion that happiness equals stimulation of the pleasure nerve, to the maintenance of a pleasant mood, to dutifully collecting and caring for our things, to gardening and having sex. And if we ever find within ourselves an instinct for something more adventurous, what do we do? We buy a 60-inch Sony and find some cheap, instant, system-approved gratification by playing *WoW* or watching *Lord of the Rings* on Blu-Ray.

3. In *The Sims* there are some questions you ask and some you don't. You *may* ask "how" type questions. For instance, "How do I (as in, your Sim) get a girlfriend?" or "How do I impress my neighbors?" These are relevant questions. These questions have simple answers. You buy expensive shoes, clothes, watches, and televisions.

---

[73] Wouldn't be the first time. I mean, if *Moses* did it...

You garden. You treat people politely, and try to get along as best you can. This is the meaning of life. Basically, you try to be Canadian.

There are other questions you don't ask. You don't ask "why" questions. You don't ask "Why am I here?" or "Why do I need to sleep?" or "Why do I need friends?" You just need to sleep. Those are the rules. In order to gain any kind of satisfaction from the game, you mustn't ask these questions.

You don't ask historical questions either. You don't ask what school you went to, who your first kiss was, or when you decided that chocolate ice cream is better than vanilla.[74] These questions do not help you answer the "how" questions, so they are not relevant.

This is how we treat other people sometimes, isn't it. We treat them like characters in a game, mere role players that fill a certain function. We don't bother to ask about their stories. We treat them as cogs in the system: beings that serve as filler characters in our simulated universe.

When was the last time you asked the McDonalds drive-through lady who her first kiss was? Try it. I dare you.[75] You'll find that real people have these entire stories to their lives that *Sim* characters don't. People are not like *Sim* characters. But I have noticed that we are begin-

---

[74] I should probably admit that this bit of the chapter is inspired by Chuck Klosterman's chapter on the same video game.. I think I stole the talking to a bush part from him as well. My bad, Chuck. Furthermore, my brother tells me that Donald Miller does a bit on this whole "how" vs. "why" question thing. I didn't know that, but to avoid sounding like I stole his ideas, I will credit him as well.

[75] Just make sure the guy in line behind you isn't driving a Hummer.

ning to act and think like them. There is a general propensity in our culture for people to play the roles of certain characters in their lives. Depending on where we are, or whom we're with, we play a "role" to a certain extent, and we're not really sure where that "role" came from.

I think this is because we live in a fractured reality: we understand that there are different worlds with different rules—different games, if you will—that we step in and out of everyday. These include the world of work, of home, of school, and of guys' poker night. Not to mention online worlds. We compensate by adopting a role that we believe will help us adapt to each situation. We play the suck up at work. The stay-at-home-wife who watches Oprah. The Emo-kid who listens to My Chemical Romance. Etc. We get really obsessed with the maintenance of these particular identities in different situations, from the one at high school to the one at the mall to the one in *World of Warcraft*, so much that we either become very unsure of who we actually are, or if there is anything to us besides what we've chosen to invest ourselves in.

Some people choose the audacious jock role—others, the meek night elf. Both are quite ridiculous. Yet we get so concerned with keeping up these roles that we have little time to think about their ridiculousness and actually invest in a deeper, more authentic self: in character. For my generation, character no longer refers to one's moral fiber. It refers to one's social identity: one's role. You don't *have* character. You *are* one.

But what happens when a whole generation loses the ability to develop good, old-fashioned character?

My brother likes to read a lot of books by this guy John Elderidge, who wrote *Wild at Heart* and a bunch of spin-offs. My brother tells me that Mr. Elderidge's main idea is that "a man has to know that he has what it takes." This is basically my brother's mantra, and he is presently in Afghanistan with the military finding the answer to that question. What exactly this statement means, I'm not sure. I suppose it means that we, and I can really only speak for myself and most other men I know, have to prove to ourselves that we can be successful in life. We need to prove to ourselves that we can make money, win over a woman, gain the approval of our friends and peers, make our dads proud, take care of a family, become a role model, build a house, and so on. This is a basic human need: for men at least. We need to find a challenge, to face that challenge, and to overcome it. This is what makes us feel like we belong. This is where we find meaning, and a happiness that lasts. This is what builds character.

This is also the deep-seated instinct that is exploited by video games in the notion of beating the game. Instead of facing the vague and daunting task of finding success in real life, it's much easier to do so in a game. It is easier to be a man in *WoW* than it is in real life. But deep within us we have a need for real knowledge, for real mystery, for a real story in which to live. We have these instincts to fight, to go on adventures, to explore the dangerous depths of a mysterious existence, and to conquer them. These instincts are built into our DNA. They make up the fabric of our humanity, a fabric that is stifled by modern methods of control that anesthetize our instincts, that blunt and discourage our desire to be like real men.

We are told to avoid adventures because they aren't safe, that we should avoid fighting because we might lose some teeth or poke someone's eye out. We are told that mystery has been conquered: that science has figured everything out. Scientific achievement, consumer society and political correctness have turned us into sleepwalking shadows of our potential selves, because there's no land left to conquer, no demon left to fight. The mission gave us meaning. But now, like in *2001: A Space Odyssey,* we're just along for the ride.

So NO WONDER we turn to the one outlet left for us to just punch some dude's face in. Video games have become a secure and safe outlet for our dangerous, politically incorrect instincts. They are not evil. But maybe these instincts aren't supposed to be controlled, suppressed, dulled, and limited to the world of virtual reality. Maybe they are supposed to be directed, channeled, and disciplined. However, when we lose touch with God, with the supernatural framework of reality, and when we start to believe that magic and mystery exist only onscreen, meaning itself slips into the abyss of foggy relativism and we lose any reason or motivation to discipline ourselves into becoming a particular kind of man. So instead of seeking out real sex, we look at I-porn. Instead of seeking out real adventure, we play *WoW.* Instead of living life, we watch others do it by pointing a mouse or a remote, because it's easier. We subscribe to the outlets the system has prescribed as acceptable. We submit to the easy outs. Instead of choosing real life, we settle for a cheap substitute. This is the danger of living a computer-mediated reality. It's easier. But it isn't better.

4. When I was in grade nine, the biggest movie around was

The Matrix. Everybody was watching it and talking about it: at the mall, at the coffee shop, and even at church. Now I'm not going to pretend I have anything new to say about this movie. In fact, since its bastardization in the early 2000's by countless church youth groups as a ploy to convert unsuspecting teenage boys—*are you going to take the red pill (culture), or the blue pill (Jesus)?*—it's just not cool to talk about anymore. Which is unfortunate, because it's a great idea.

The premise of the film is this: the computers need us to survive. So in order to keep us plugged in, they convince the humans that we need computers to be alive: or to *feel* alive, rather.[76] We become dependent upon 'the system' for our survival, and eventually, the lines of humanity are blurred with those of the machine.

In the advertising campaign behind this film, they didn't want anyone to know what *The Matrix* was. Like the protagonist of the film, audiences were left in the dark, left to figure it out for themselves. The big idea was that the movie would become a talking point around the water cooler: "hey, so, do *you* know what *The Matrix* is?"

Well, in the film, the actual matrix was a mainframe run by AI that used humans as batteries. In real life, there is a system like this, too: though it's not so theatrical in appearance, and we aren't literally plugged in to it.

I've used this word 'the system' a lot. You've probably heard it elsewhere, too: a word that can mean almost anything and everything: the 'man,' the corporation, the hive-mind. Let me propose something else: the system is a way of doing culture that understands and treats people a certain way. I believe it began with a man named Machiavelli.

---

[76] One character argues that they feel more alive inside the Matrix than outside it. That steak tastes better inside, and the sex is better, and so on.

The 'system' is a way of running society that subscribes to the ideas of the political philosopher Machiavelli, who, as Leo Strauss describes,

> rejects the whole philosophic and theological tradition... (He believes) one must start from how men do live; one must lower one's sights. The immediate corollary is the reinterpretation of virtue: virtue must not be understood as that for the sake of which the commonwealth exists, but virtue exists exclusively for the sake of the commonwealth... The political problem becomes a technical problem... the fundamental political problem is simply one of "a good organization of the state.[77]

As philosophers reasoned that politics could never make men good, governments stopped trying to encourage virtue, and started to encourage conformity. This makes us easier to control. Governments started treating people like things: things to be calculated, predicted, and manipulated. The best state, it was argued, is one that uses simple techniques rather than virtue to guarantee survival and success. And gradually, we gave in, high on the narcotic of comfort and pleasure, gladly surrendering our individuality for a fake replica, selling our souls to gain the (virtual) world.

---

[77] Leo Strauss "The Three Waves of Modernity," from *An Introduction to Political Philosophy: Ten Essays by Leo Strauss*, ed. Hilail Gildin (Detroit: Wayne State University Press, 1989)

Thus, it became irrelevant for people to try to be good, moral, and righteous. The most productive members of the state were merely predictable. And our vices are much more predictable than our virtues. And so, what is the real world version of *The Matrix,* really? It is a set of principles bred in the minds of greedy men that guide our politics, economy and education by aiming to keep us predictable.

If you understand how to predict a man's desires and offer him quick and easy satisfaction, you can make a lot of money. Just ask the people who run the billion dollar porn industry. They, along with companies like Microsoft and Apple, try to convince us that our desires are best met onscreen. They are trying to convince us that it is only possible to be human, to *feel* like a human, when you're on the computer.

And they've succeeded, haven't they. They've convinced us that we *need* computers. They know that humans are social beings. We need relationships to survive. So not only do computers mediate most of our relationships through email and Facebook, but they go one further. Many people, I'm sure, would describe the relationships they have with their personal computers as just that: a relationship. A computer is more than a tool, like a simple pair of scissors. It is more like a person, only much better in many ways. It doesn't judge you. It's always there for you. It's full of interesting perspectives on things. It's much more entertaining. *And* it's easier to turn on.[78]

In fact, in many ways, computers are better friends than people. We may not admit this belief, but we prove it with our practice. We trust computers with our greatest secrets: passwords, journals, browsing his-

---

[78] *double entendre* alert!

tory. We spend more time on computers than with other people. We meet other people and uphold our identities through online social networks using computers. They also facilitate most of our everyday activi-activities: reading, communicating, shopping, entertainment. We live computer-mediated lives. Without them, we become disconnected, un-enlightened, frightened and anxious beings. Without them, we're not sure what to do with ourselves. Truly, today, becoming computer-literate is a necessary step in becoming human.[79]

Lately this "new way to be human"[80] has been shown to have some frightening consequences. In Ontario not long ago, a young boy ran away from home and committed suicide because his parents took his Xbox 360 (a Microsoft made machine that effortlessly combines game console with the characteristics of a computer, such as a hard drive and internet capabilities) away. They might as well have severed an artery. By cutting their son off from his virtual community of friends, from his role as leader of a clan in *Halo 3,* and essentially from the things he val-ued most in life, they cut him off from the source to which he clung desperately for meaning. I suppose that living in this *Sims*-esque mind numbing, spirit crushing meaningless post-modern existence is not without its hazards.

---

[79] "Perhaps there's no such thing as an authentic self. Maybe Walt Whitman was right: We contain multitudes. Part child, part adult. Androgynes. Cyborgs. We understand in-tuitively that machines are becoming more like humans, and now via the promise of virtual reality we have the opportunity to meet machines halfway." – Kalle Lasn, *Culture Jam*

[80] To borrow a phrase from Charlie Peacock and Switchfoot and perhaps countless oth-ers.

There are dozens of people I know or have heard about through the grape vine who spend nearly all of their free time and invest all sorts of mental energy in *WoW* or *Halo*, thereby alienating themselves from people in "RL." They are committed to sharpening their characters and gaming skills so much that basic life and social skills deteriorate rapidly. Have you ever tried to have a conversation about philosophy or art with a *WoW* addict? It's not pretty. Like a drug addict, their focus is directed at one thing, and cannot shift from that direction for very long. If you'd like to have some fun, just mention "The Sword of a Thousand Truths"[81] to a level 47 *WoW* addict and watch the spectacle of incoherent drivel[82] that bursts forth like a hot spring.

This is the most clear and present danger that video games introduce. Not desensitization to violence. Not poor eating habits. Not the occasional indulgence in escapism from time to time. There is nothing wrong, in my mind, with the occasional game of *Tetris*, *Madden* or even *Halo*. But when we start to seek fulfillment for our deeper, human instincts within the world of computer mediated fictional reality, where responsibilities are easily ignored, it dulls the experience of real life. It can consume you, like a drug. And like a true addict, you look to your addiction for salvation from the very problems it creates.

---

[81] To be fair, I learned of this from the South Park *WoW* episode, and am not entirely sure if it really exists, but I suspect it does.

[82] Side note: Drivel is perhaps the most interesting word to look up in a Thesaurus. Some of its synonyms include codswallop, guff, bunkum, flapdoodle and piffle. *Yes*. Piffle.

5. We look to computers to make us feel more human: to

give us simulated satisfaction of our desires. I can imagine a day when all of our needs—social, emotional and sexual—will be met by exclusively by computers. I can tell that this is already happening. Many *WoW* aficionados live computer mediated lives with computer mediated friends, colleagues, and even spouses (yes, you can get married in the *World of Warcraft*). The real people behind these identities don't seem to matter. It's their online characters that are important. Our real selves, in these worlds, are not important. Character, integrity, and virtue are frivolous words in virtual reality. What really matters is skill. The boundaries that separate real life from virtual reality are becoming more obscure. Character and integrity are becoming frivolous words in real life as well. I think that when we blur the boundaries between our offline and online identities, when we favor the skill of efficient multitasking over virtue, we begin to sacrifice our independence, and our humanity.

Maybe *WoW* foreshadows a time when computers will replace our friends and our spouses. That may seem a little too 80's sci-fi for you, but who knows? Maybe one day we will happily trade our old, decaying human friends for shiny new models that will never die or hurt our feelings. Maybe we'll prefer they be controlled by actual humans, but maybe we won't care, or notice the difference. Perhaps one day, I will be able to fulfill my dream of having an entourage, a computer-friend for every need I might have. It's not that far off, really. We already keep an entourage of gadgets. Why not an entourage of robots? If Shia Labeouf can have one, why can't I?[83]

Some people I know can't live apart from constant contact with their entourage of laptops, iPhone, TV's and Playstations. If they went twenty-four hours without electronic stimulation, they'd go into withdrawal. I'm not sure that I'd do much better. Would you? I imagine it's possible that one day you'll be able to get your iPhone sewn into your arm, or attached to your hip, so you'll never have to go without it. And the worst will have happened. Our nightmare will have come true. The human race will have evolved into a new, frightening species. Man will be abolished, as C.S. Lewis, Firedrake Nietzsche[84] and James Cameron predicted, and we will emerge as a race of indifferent, lazy, self-obsessed cyborgs.

It's not as strange as you might think. After all, the definition of a cyborg is "a person whose physiological functioning is aided by or dependent upon a mechanical or electronic device."[85] This seems like an accurate description of many people I know. As well, I'm sure that if we had our cell phones implanted in our brains, and had constant Twitter updates from everyone in the world, we'd pretty much achieve omniscience. The people at Apple probably believe this is a realistic dream. One

---

[83] Confused? Go watch *Transformers*. Or don't. Ya, that's probably a better idea.

[84] My spell check auto-corrected the name of one of the greatest philosophers of all time, and I submitted to its wrathful will. One day, perhaps we'll trust auto-correct so much that to change it or add new words will amount to blasphemy.

[85] The Dictionary.com definition

day, they will call us "almighty ruler" like Burger King does, only they might actually be able to facilitate such a thing.

In this case, all education will become irrelevant. Why bother memorizing new facts, like the events and ideas that built America, when we have constant contact with Wikipedia? Why bother to learn a new skill like playing the piano when we'll be able to download new skills by plugging wires into our heads like in... nevermind.[86] Why bother making new friends in reality, where you actually have to talk to them, when you can find someone much more interesting to befriend on MyFace, with whom you can communicate exclusively in LOL-speak and emoticons?

If we don't give computers control of our actual bodies, we will likely give them control of everything else. We will become so dependent upon computers, and so trusting of them, that we will offer them control willingly. We'll find contentment in delegating our work to them, while we wait around to die. Growing fat, dumb and complacent, like the people on the cruise ship in *Wall-E*. Either that, or we'll turn into the Borg.

As we surrender control to the great system of super-computers, what is lost? Our society is becoming more and more dependent on a system of organization and economics that thinks like a computer. Its goal is to keep us calm, cool and collected, faithfully plugging away at our jobs, fueling the economy by purchasing toys for our kids and gadg-

---

[86] Oops, I almost made a reference to the movie that shall not be named for the sake of its excessive metaphorical overuse in the early '00's by Christian youth pastors trying to be hip.

ets for ourselves, driving a system whose utmost priority is self-preservation. Sounds kind of like we are the ones being used, like batteries, just like in… you know. Society is no longer just a group of people. It's become a bureaucratic machine of political preservation and technological wizardry. And we need to rage against the machine, people! We need to take it back! Where's Zach de la Rocha[87] when you need him?

You might think I'm overreacting, but I'm not. Face it: The synthetic eco-system in which you live treats you like a *Sim*. It doesn't care where you came from, or what your story is, or who "the real you" is. It doesn't care if your character is good, or evil. It just wants you to buy into its system, so that you'll work really hard at your soul-crushing nine-to-five to pay off the credit card bills you racked up on those shoes you just *had* to have because you *knew* they would make Chad take you back and make all your friends jealous. It wants to keep you blissfully unaware of how it shapes your soul and steers the trajectory of the human race through the subtle, everyday submission it invites.

The system wants you to believe that happiness is what it tells you: or rather, what it *sells* you. It wants you to believe that you aren't good enough as you are: that you need bleached teeth, a shiny cell phone and a sleek car. It wants you to stop wanting to be *you*, and start wanting to be someone else. It wants you to believe that this is how the game is played: that this is how existence works. Because this is what keeps us buying, and in turn, what makes the system run. It needs us to stay plugged in: to play the games it makes for us: to pretend we are *The Sims*, and let the system program and control us via our basic instincts.

---

[87] Lead singer of the anarchy-preaching aptly named band *Rage Against the Machine*.

What's most unnerving is that it has succeeded, for the most part. This is who we have become: self-absorbed, pleasure-obsessed caricatures of a morally inept species who harbor little concern for the wider world or the future to come.

This is a crucial episode in the history of mankind. And it falls on us to set things right: to take up the real life *quest* of rescuing our humanity. This is our mission: our task. To respond with our lives to the words of Alexis de Tocqueville, a French philosopher, who warned more than a century ago,

> Most of the people in these [democratic] nations are extremely eager in the pursuit of immediate material pleasures and are always discontented with the position they occupy and always free to leave it. They think about nothing but ways of changing their lot and better-ing it. For people in this frame of mind every new way of getting wealth more quickly, every machine which lessens work, every means of diminishing the costs of production, every invention which makes pleasures eas-ier or greater, seems the most magnificent accomplishment of the human mind....

> The prospect really does frighten me that they may finally become so engrossed in a cowardly love of im-mediate pleasures that their interest in their own future and in that of their descendants may vanish, and that they will prefer tamely to follow the course of their des-

tiny rather than make a sudden energetic effort necessary to set things right.[88]

Imagine what he'd write if he were alive today. Truly, we run
the risk of inviting limitless future scorn by carelessly spoiling the environment, recklessly depleting our resources, cutting our ties with
tradition through cultural elitism and obscuring the meaning and duties
as humans. Not to mention the personal problems we create through addictions to escapism. *All because we choose to just play along*—like a
player of, and a character in, a video game. The simple truth is that in
order to set things right—in order to protect *what truly makes us human*—you can't play *The Sims* forever.

---

[88] Toqueville, *Letters to America*

An excerpt from the blog of Justin Vernon (aka Bon Iver) on BonIver.org, after watching the 2011 MTV video awards show, entitled, "some shit I just gotta say about last night." Posted August 29, 2011.

"Can i just ask, the reader, us, we ... as non-rhetorically as possible: don't we seem dumb? didn't MTV lose the fight against themselves? Didn't Rock'n'Roll STOP? Why are the lights so bright? isn't our talent as artists enough? Why do we try SO hard? Does a moonman mean what it did back then? Should we feel pumped when we get one? Should our mom's cry? I am not even thinking about it that hard. I will close my eyes in 90 seconds and have total peace... But, seriously. Why are we waving around so much? Why do we NEED this shit so bad? Why don't we just have MUSIC? DO music? soul? I don't know. I don't mean to criticize. Anyone. Actually. Except for MTV. You might have had a very large opportunity to stabilize yourself as a global presence of culture and art about 15 years ago and you f****** the dog. Sorry. I'm with my girls on this one. Its becoming increasingly clear as I think about it more and more, that the dollars, if they ARE apart of why you are doing something... they are apart of why you are doing something. that's f***** to me. **that's the absence of spirit, glue, fabric of what makes us a person.** it distracts us from what we could be doing: WORK. on EARTH."

(edited for emphasis)

Five.

On Music
Or, *Here's to You, Nickleback*
(MTV vs. Art)

Recommended Listening: your own favorite album—on record.

Or *Kid A* by Radiohead.

"Come writers and critics

Who prophesy with your pen

And keep your eyes wide

The chance won't come again

And don't speak too soon

For the wheel's still in spin

And there's no tellin' who

That it's namin'.

For the loser now

Will be later to win

For the times they are a-changin'."

116

- Bob Dylan, *The Times they are a-Changin'*

"I just don't think it's as epic as *OK*," he said matter-of-factly.

"No," I shot back, "It's beyond epic. It takes you to the frightening end of familiarity, beyond happy endings, or even predictable
endings. It's like visiting another dimension."

"Yeah, well, I still think you're wrong. *OK* was the better album."

"Wanna fight?"

So a while back, I had an argument—well, more like a series of
escalating rhetorical uppercuts—with my friend Zach about the 'importance' of Radiohead's 2001 album *Kid A* vs. their 1997 offering *OK
Computer*. Yeah, we have lives. These two albums, we agreed, represent
the creative culmination of rock music in the last century. But agree-
ment doesn't make for interesting conversation, so we argued over
which was better.

I conceded that *OK Computer* may feature some fantastically epic songs like "Airbag" and "Lucky," but argued that, "*Kid A* is more
"important," because of its peculiar originality and seamless unity. It
weaves a sonic storyboard of hauntingly beautiful emotional landscapes,
and invites listeners to traverse at their own peril. It better embodies the
shadowy nature of existence than any other album I can think of. *Kid A*
summons listeners to reflect upon their experiences of the tension between order and chaos in their own lives, and in doing so, offers an
unflinchingly sober perspective on life itself, one that walks a fine line
between despairing resignation and hopeful optimism. *That* is why *Kid
A* is so damn important. *Bi-otch!*"

Zach disagreed. "*OK Computer* has a more relevant social commentary, which, combined with its rebellion against the grunge-rock template while making a one last stand for the 'concept' album, makes it more important."

"Wait," I replied. "So you aren't arguing that *OK* is better just because you *like* it more, but because you think it is *objectively better?*"

"I guess."

"Well, *I* guess we can agree that both albums are *objectively* better than pretty much any others released in the last fifteen years."

"Yes."

"But *Kid A* is better."

"You think *Kid A* is better, I think *OK* is better. Let's not beat each other up over it."

But instead of defaulting to sensitive passivity, I countered, "No. We *should* be fighting over it. Men have always fought to the death over meaningless differences in opinion. One guy would say something like (invoke Sideshow Mel accent here), "My horse is better looking than yours!" And the other would reply, "Perhaps, but mine is better trained!" Then the one would slap the other with a white glove, muster his pride, and snort, "I challenge you to a DU-EL!" Then someone would die of a gunshot wound, or at least lose a limb.

This was a part of being a man: fighting for your pride, for your beliefs. And if anything is worth fighting over—besides women or land—it's music. "So put up your dukes, son!"

What followed wasn't pretty. There is a reason that boxers and wrestlers don't use "Fake Plastic Trees" as their theme music.

According to my blurry recollection of history, this is how men settled things: with clubs, swords, guns, or fast cars. Exactly when we became "civilized" and stopped these things, I'm not sure. But I do know that, however violent they were, these actions made up a vital part of the human experience, as they helped you learn to stand up for yourself and your beliefs.

I imagine that in a duel, you'd find out what you're really made of. You'd learn to stare into death's penetrating eyes and hold a level gaze. In moments like these, I imagine you'd feel truly alive. But this doesn't happen much anymore. We don't duel anymore. We don't even argue. Today, we're "civilized." We're "nice." We're "tolerant."

This is why I hate tolerance. Ever since we became "tolerant," not only did we stop fighting, we pretty much stopped arguing. At least, about the important things. Most people I know don't really stand up for their beliefs. We've all but forgotten how. So, for once, I am going to take a stand, and proclaim to the world my perhaps "intolerant" belief that the world needs more music snobs,[89] like Zach and me.

How to be a Music Snob:
Lesson #1: Snobs argue about music.

When Zach and I went toe to toe, I noticed it was the first time I'd argued about something "trivial" like music for a long time. And yet, it felt so *right.* As far as I know, Radiohead fans are the only ones who still argue about things like the "importance" of certain rock bands, or about rock mu-

[89] I realize this word means different things to different people, but I'm referring to the Seth Cohen or Chuck Klosterman template of music snob, not the bourgeoisie Chopin and Mozart kind of music snob.

sic itself. It used to be all the rage in the '60s, the decade where Rock came of age, at least as far as I can tell from documentaries and books. Apparently, people used to read *Rolling Stone* magazine, like, all the time, and its articles were more than filler underneath glossy shots of a shirtless John Mayer.

Instead, they were bound by a severe journalistic integrity that took the social role of music seriously.[90] As well, most radio DJ's felt their utmost duty was to the listener, not record companies or advertisers. People expected more from their favorite musician than just harmonies and guitar licks, and musicians themselves provided more than mere entertainment. They provided leadership. They offered a soundtrack to a social revolution.

As people gradually stopped arguing about horses and war and politics, rock music became the last bastion for clashes of opinion rooted firmly in hubris. People felt *proud* that they liked certain bands, and disliked others, and felt the need to share their opinions. Loudly. People weren't proud merely because they *preferred* one band to the next. They were also proud because they thought one band or musician "more important" than the next, and hence, deserved more devotion. Bands were judged on everything from musical cues to songwriting ability to the legitimacy of a song's message, which naturally led into an argument over government policies or religious freedom or the best form of social revolution. Music was a medium for the expression of important ideas: controversial, world-changing ideas. The renegade rock star mold was

---

[90] For an articulation of RS's devolution to *Maxim* wannabe, see "Literary 'Rolling Stone' sells out to male titillation" USA Today, Date TK, 2002. Not sure how that works out with the John Mayer photo's though.

first rooted in a rebellion not against graying social mores, but in protest rallies against the Vietnam War, the Bomb, and Racism. Music was an arena where we fought for peace and human rights. It was *important*.

Sure, in the 60's, popular music was on a steady trend towards purely commercial uses. But some, like Bob Dylan, stood bravely in opposition, and served as a rallying point for others. As one writer notes,

> The protest songs that made Dylan famous and with
> which he continues to be associated were … influ-
> enced by American radical traditions and above all by
> the political ferment touched off among young people
> by the civil rights and ban the bomb movements, he
> engaged in his songs with the terror of the nuclear arms
> race, with poverty, racism and prison, jingoism and
> war.[91]

Bob Dylan understood that music was a medium for the expression of ideas that could challenge the propaganda of governments and corporations and unite the people in loyalty against them. Dylan "found himself crowned as the laureate of a social movement, hailed as 'the voice of a generation.'"[92] His was a generation that, if nothing else, found a worldview, and an identity, in their music. It united them. Again—it was *important*.

---

[91] Marqusee, Mike. "The Politics of Bob Dylan." *Red Pepper*. Red Pepper, Nov. 2003. Web. 07 Sept. 2011. <http://www.redpepper.org.uk/The-Politics-of-Bob-Dylan/>.
[92] Ibid.

In those days, listening to music was a shared experience. When someone bought a new record, she'd invite others to come over and listen to it—to soak in it. Then, in the summers, she'd invite her friends to drive countless hours so they could go to big concerts like Woodstock and listen with other people. They understood that music provided not just an experience, but also a worldview. It was a lifestyle of revolution. Even The Beatles were in on the act:

> You say you want a Revolution?
> Well, you know,
> we all want to change the world.[93]

Popular music once gave us a reason to change the world. And now we listen to whiny top 40 songs on our iPods that have nothing to do with real life or politics or protests and have generally nothing important to talk about but love and sex and teen angst. Popular music doesn't unite us anymore; it separates us. It doesn't challenge the status quo; it reinforces it. It doesn't inspire us to really change things. There is something frightfully wrong with the music we currently listen to, and the ways that we listen to it. This is why the world needs more music snobs, to serve as protectors: as prophets to remind the world that music is about *more* than just music, and that Music. Is. *Important.*

Lesson #2: Snobs don't listen to "everything."

---

[93] from *Revolution*. I can't help but hear Jim Sturgess' heavily auto-tuned, *Across the Universe* rendition echo through my skull, drowning out the original.

Whenever I'm forced to make awkward conversation with a stranger at a party or laundromat, my go-to question is usually this: "So, what bands are you into right now?" I've found that many people give the same response: "Oh, you know, *everything*. Except ------- (insert "Country" if it's a boy or "Heavy Metal" if it's a girl)."

At the risk of offending half of my readership, people who give this answer suck. If you ever happen to make my acquaintance and I offer this reply to your humble query, please sucker-punch me in the spleen. This answer is lame because,

A: You do not listen to everything. You probably listen to old sentimental favorites and Top 40, which is to *real* music as the Star Wars Holiday Special is to the original trilogy. [94]

B: You like music, but don't think that it is important enough to think deeply about it, and choose your loyalties to certain artists carefully.

C: In giving this answer, you reveal yourself to be an uncivilized peon with all the cultural awareness of a mallard duck.

Nobody should ever say that they listen to "everything but country/heavy metal." This is wrong. And I'll tell you why. Because when you give this answer, you relinquish your right—nay, your *duty*—to keep artists accountable to their art form, and thus, to civilization. It is *your* duty to remind artists that a song is not a commercial. And so, it is your duty to your country, even to civilization itself, to be a music snob.

---

[94] They should put *that* analogy on the SAT.

The other day I saw Avril Lavigne in a Nikon ad. A few minutes later, I heard Justin Timberlake singing the McDonalds' song. Then Beyoncé came on, telling me to buy some Maybelline. Then Jessica Simpson tried to sell me acne medication. And so on. It worries me that the most popular artists on the continent have an obvious agenda to sell me fast food and make-up. It worries me because these are, whether we like it or not, what I just said: our most popular *artists*.

What is an artist? It's a weird question, because we will answer it differently depending on the time frame. If you ask about artists in the 15th century, you might get an answer about painters and sculptors, about people who were hand picked, trained, and encouraged to create truly beautiful pieces that would become priceless treasures. The social role of the artist was to push the bounds of human creativity, to teach people about historical events and figures, and sometimes, to push back against the dominant cultural forces in society. Painters did it. Architects did it. And musicians did it. Good art was, perhaps, the greatest expression of the human spirit, because it transcended culture. It revealed truth, and beauty: the mysterious, glorious reality that exists all around us, but is often very hard to notice, because we've become so used to staring right through it.

Excellent art is a part of our heritage. But nowadays, I can't name even one painter, architect, or sculptor that is still breathing. But I *can* name various musicians, actors, and movie directors. These are *our* artists. Today, art as a genre has been largely distilled into forms of film and music. However, instead of trying to push the bounds of creativity, or helping us notice truth, record labels and Hollywood have teamed up to coax us into a haze of blissful submission to the propaganda of consumerism. Art has been co-opted by businessmen. Now, instead of letting it challenge us, we demand that art entertain us. In the process, good art becomes harder to unearth, and its historical role to play in our culture becomes all but obsolete.

Now that we look to art for entertainment over education, the role of the critic has been lost. As fewer and fewer people pay attention to music critics, musicians have become like children without supervision, free to create without threat of stern rebuke from critics *or* audiences; free from accountability to the spirit of their art. The only standard popular artists hold themselves to is this: ***will it sell?*** Most top 40 veterans have ceased to care about responsibility to the craft and tradition of rock music, and music at large. To the tradition of art, and it's ability to evoke the transcendent. So here's to you, Nickleback, Eminem and Lady Gaga, and all of your fans. Because when you turn art into something to be mass produced for commercial purposes, you treat music as something to be consumed rather than something to be treasured, appreciated and protected. You willingly forsake the power that art holds to challenge us, and to change us.

Our only hope to change this pattern is to begin to pay attention to what we listen to: to the artists we support. Is this or that band merely trying to sell records, or do they have an agenda to create good art that helps us explore the meaning of what it means to be human? This may seem like a lofty goal for Kelly Clarkson, but it's the task that artists have always been charged with. Why should she be off the hook? The truth is if we want to protect music's ability to teach us, to connect us with meaning, we should listen to anything[95] but "everything."

Lesson #3: Snobs listen to records.

I was fortunate enough to visit the Louvre in Paris a couple years ago. Since I was by myself, I unwittingly brought my iPod along. As I wandered through the first hall and up the stairs, I noticed a guy of a similar age who was also wearing white ear buds like a fashion state-ment. I imagined the scolding my grandparents would have given him. "Have some *respect*, you half-wit." I quickly pulled mine out and stuffed them in my pocket. Leonardo Da Vinci probably didn't think the Mona Lisa needed a soundtrack. I can respect that.

As I pushed my way through the dense crowd to lock eyes with Mona, I overheard a number of conversations. Most were variations of the same thing: "What is she smiling about?" It's a question people have asked themselves for generations. In asking this question, you partici-pate in a conversation that has occurred for five hundred years. You become part of a tradition. You see that the importance of a painting like this doesn't lie in its brush strokes or palette, but in its place in the larger story of civilization. I couldn't help but feel a connection to history, and to my fellow man, mediated by this symbolic piece of art. And just then, my thoughts were interrupted by some dude behind me who muttered, "Wow, thirty Euros for this? Big deal." Then he stuck his headphones

---

[95] Anything, meaning Radiohead and Bob Dylan.

on and walked away. How quickly he was to dismiss something so culturally important, just because it didn't suit his need to feel entertained.

There is a reason they put great pieces of art in museums. They do this so people can share their viewing experiences with friends, neighbors, and strangers. When a piece of art is experienced outside of community, it loses part of its intended function. It gives itself over to any crazy interpretation we might, in our solitude, give it. This is why my dependence on my iPod, and its incredible popularity with my generation, worries me. We don't really listen to music in groups, anymore. We don't get together with our friends to listen to records. We listen to iPods. We listen to music in solitude.

How does this affect us? Well, I am used to interpreting meaning via sound cues, like in movies. By allowing me to paint any moment with the soundtrack of any of a thousand songs, my iPod offers me the ability to control my interpretation of any given experience: it subconsciously reinforces the belief that the world is all about me.

As I thought about this in the Louvre, I recalled an argument from a book I read in university, called *The Closing of the American Mind*. Author Allan Bloom says of kids these days, and their music, "as long as they have the Walkman on, (they) cannot hear what the great tradition has to say and, after its prolonged use, when they take it off, they find they are deaf."[96]

Basically, he's saying that music helps us disengage from the real world, and if we do it long enough, we become unable to reengage.

---

[96] Bloom, *Closing of the American Mind.* 81

We find that we are addicted to seeing the world as mere sensation—as it appears to us when we have rock blaring through our headphones.

I laughed at this the first time I read it. Now I wish I could disagree with him. When I listen to my Walkman... er... iPod, the world is at my disposal. I can color different moments with any one of a thousand songs that may serve as portals to distant emotions. Boredom becomes bearable, and even good experiences are heightened when accompanied by the perfect song. But when I don't have my iPod, when I can't color each moment with sound, I feel like something's missing.

I admit it. I am addicted to music's ability to make my life seem meaningful. I am addicted to the feeling it gives me that I am the centre of the universe, and that nothing else matters. I am addicted to its ability to help me escape. I wonder how many times I've uttered "big deal" towards something like the Mona Lisa, or towards life itself, simply because it didn't suit my desire to be entertained.

Now, I love my iPod like I love few other things in this world. It is pure majesty to have access to thousands of songs at any given moment without lugging around a satchel filled to the brim with CD cases. However, I am slowly realizing that without my iPod, my experience of the world seems less colorful, and less interesting. With my headphones on, I am less aware of the world and how I fit into it. They help me to disengage—to become viewer, rather than participant. Instead of actually living a more significant life, I become satisfied with *feeling* like I'm living a more significant life. Perhaps it's because I want my life to look like a movie, and if I can't find true love and defeat my sworn enemy in under two hours, I should at least find a decent soundtrack that makes it *feel* like I can.

Music, however, is not supposed to help you escape by making life seem more entertaining. It is *art*, after all. And art is not there just to be hung on the wall because it looks nice. It isn't there to make us feel better about ourselves, or our world. It is not there to help us transcend our reality.

Maybe you need to hear that again.

The function of art is not to help us 'transcend' reality. It is there to *show* us reality.

True art is able to strip the varnish of familiarity from the mundane in order to reveal something glorious: to reveal true beauty, and true emotion.

Good art does not make up transcendence. It reveals transcendence. It isn't there to make us feel like we have more important lives than we actually do. It's there to show us that our lives are actually pretty important—that the things we do *have* importance—and that we should strive to do important things.

So maybe, instead of supporting musicians that just want to sell records, I should start supporting artists that are trying to say something important—that are pointing me towards truth. That are trying to say something new. That are describing difficult emotions, or questioning our comfortable worldview.

And instead of just listening to music on my iPod, I need to listen to it in other ways, let it connect me with other people, rather than disconnect me from them. Maybe I need should go to more concerts, buy actual records and listen to them with friends, or stop and listen to that guy busking on a sidewalk. Because when we experience music with other people, we are reminded that the world is not all about me, and that music isn't there to help me escape... it's there to teach me, to teach *us*, how to really live.

Lesson #4: Music snobs only date other music snobs.

I first became aware of what my iPod was doing to me that day in the Louvre, but the feeling grew more acute the day I left Europe. You see, whenever I get on a plane, I place my ear-buds firmly where they belong: in my ears. Inevitably, the stewardess will ask me to take them out, because listening to music on a plane will cause it to explode, I guess. But I will usually slouch down and slip them back into my ears, keeping a keen eye on the warden as she makes her way further down the aisle, reminding everyone to put their seats and table trays in the upright and locked position. Like a true child of rock, I am such a rebel.

At times like these, I need my music. Every time the plane takes off, I feel a rush of excitement and drama, like my life is an adventure movie, and someone is drawing a red line to my destination, like in an *Indiana Jones* flick. Moments like these call for the perfect song. So, just before every takeoff, I choose a song that best expresses the weighty significance of my cross-country flight. I choose one, like Mew's "Comforting Sounds," and feel the adrenaline flow as I am lifted into the sky. For a few moments, my life is a story worth telling.

That is, until the stewardess scolds me, or shoots a frigid stare that implies "You are not special. You are a humble peon like everyone else. Follow the damn rules." In which case, I sulk as I'm forced to endure the shrill baby cries and roaring engines like everyone else. Flying *sucks*.[97]

So I was on this plane from Amsterdam to Vancouver after my first Europe trip, and I had one of those moments worth noting in a diary, if I had one. There was this cute French-Canadian attendant who sat face to face with me during takeoff and landing. I had an exit row seat by the central bathrooms, and she was assigned to my section. I thanked my lucky stars, and wondered if this was fate—if we'd end up getting married and having kids. We'd argue over where we should live, and what religion we'd raise the children, and what curtains to buy. I wondered if she believed in God. With those brown eyes and mildly freckled skin, maybe it didn't matter.

Since I *was* under direct supervision and didn't want to be scolded again, I spent the time trying to wrestle my sanity from the shrieking baby two rows back. I freaking *hate* babies sometimes. Once we leveled out, I tried to strike up a conversation with her. Since we were pretty much sitting face to face, it seemed like a first date, complete with the usual awkward periods of silence, forced small talk and trips to the restroom.

Just after takeoff, I asked why I wasn't allowed to listen to music. I argued that we should be allowed to listen to music during takeoff

---

[97] see Chapter Two.

and landing, because these moments make our lives feel more dramatic than usual, and they deserve a decent soundtrack to wring them of their fullest potential. She disagreed. "Safety first!"

The worst phrase in the English lexicon.

I guess sometimes we are supposed to experience life like everyone else, to confront uncomfortable realities without the option for escape. Maybe it's good for me. Maybe it helps me realize that life is not all about me, and I am not the lead character in an epic-*RomCom*-adventure movie.

Changing the subject, I tried to explain my "importance of rock" thesis to the stewardess through the jet engines and incessant beeping. She seemed half-interested, and obliged with the occasional nod. Then she asked if she could take a look at my iPod. She might as well have asked to look at my soul.

As she perused my meticulously crafted playlists, she admitted she didn't know many of the bands (BTW, music snobs take a certain pride in this). I hoped she wouldn't ask about the hefty Michael W. Smith collection. Then she exclaimed, "Oh, you listen to Coldplay! I love Coldplay!" *Viva La Vida* had just been released, and I'd illegally downloaded it before my trip. After a few listens, I decided I was over Coldplay. Not wanting to offend, I concurred. "Yeah, they're great. Have you seen them in concert? Great show."

Of course, this caused my heart to sink. You see, you can tell a lot about a person based on the music they listen to. In fact, to music snobs, this is pretty much the make or break element of a relationship.

Even if you have absolutely nothing else in common, if you can agree to pump "Everything in its Right Place"[98] while driving at night, it will all mysteriously work out.

Now the trouble with a girl who likes Coldplay, as our old friend Chuck Klosterman says, is that you'll never truly satisfy her. This is because Coldplay subconsciously convinces every female fan that an unre-unrealistic idea of love is possible: that someday she'll find her own charming Brit to sing poetry to her in beautiful falsetto while skipping down a beach at sunrise, shirtless.[99]

I am not that man. No man is that man.

Chris Martin himself is not that man. Women just think he is. As Chuck says, "Coldplay manufactures fake love as frenetically as the Ford $%*#king Motor Company manufactures Mustangs." But this, Mel Gibson, is what women *really* want: "fake love." An idea. Not a reality.

Of course, Coldplay is not the only band that manufactures this ideal. It is possible to learn something important about a woman, and whether she would be a good mate, based purely on what she listens to. As established, we know that if she listens to Coldplay, she has an unrealistic idea of love, and you will never truly satisfy her. As well, if she listens to Hillsongs or Chris Tomlin, she is in love with Jesus, and you will never truly satisfy her. If she listens to Lady Gaga or Avril Lavigne, you will not be enough fun for her, and you will never truly satisfy her. If she listens to hip-hop, she probably likes to dance, and if you are white and awkward like me, you will never truly satisfy her. If she lis-

---

[98] By Radiohead, from *Kid A*, of course.

[99] See the video for "Yellow."

tens to Hannah Montana or Justin Bieber, you are far too old for her, and it wouldn't matter even if you could satisfy her, because that would be illegal. However, if she listens to *Radiohead*, she is a probably a bit of a cynic, and though you will still never truly satisfy her, that's ok, because she doesn't expect you to. She knows that nothing else in the world will ever live up to Radiohead, including your relationship.

Just another reason why Radiohead is the best.

As I pondered whether a Coldplay fan would make for a good mate, I realized the inevitability that nearly any girl I will ever date will probably hold a secret desire to be with Chris Martin. And so I will always harbor distrust towards him, and his music, and music itself, because it won't unite us. Instead, it will bifurcate our expectations of life and perspectives of reality, because in every intimate moment we share, she'll be comparing it to the first time she heard "The Scientist," while I'll be thinking of "Optimistic"—"try the best you can, the best you can is good enough."[100]

To bring it all together, remember that this is what music is used for, today: for helping you to customize each experience with your own preferred soundtrack. Except, in this case, it is actually making my reality worse, because I am being held subject to someone *else's* Coldplay-bred escapist notion that life is all about her, and that it should always live up to the way she sees it in her head when Coldplay is playing. In those moments, the music of today reveals its true colors. It has betrayed its legacy. Instead of bringing us together, uniting us in a moment, and

---

[100] More *Kid A*

134

in a worldview, it facilitates division. It breeds disappointment. Real life can never live up to the fantasy of "Fix You."[101]

This is why most popular bands, like Nickleback and Coldplay, have nothing important to contribute to the progression of human civilization, and also why music snobs don't listen to them. They do not heighten the human experience. They cheapen it. They do not open portals to a uniting experience of reality. They facilitate addictions to fake fun, and fake love. The tragedy of my relationship with Cute French-Girl would have been that the only song we'd agree to score an intimate moment would be "Fix You." Not *all* bad, but my "companionship" would never live up to the climax of the song, and she'd always be disappointed in me, because she isn't used to the oft-disappointing nature of reality as imbued in the songs of Radiohead. Of course, this was much too complicated and potentially depressing to explain to Cute French-Girl, so I racked my brain for another conversation topic.

I wanted to talk about something—anything!—but, for some reason, couldn't wrestle my mind from thinking about plane crashes. Not the best conversation starter given the circumstances. In particular, I was thinking about what song would best serve as a soundtrack to my tragic demise. "Talk Show Host"[102] probably.

---

[101] I could actually debate this with myself. In a religious context, *Fix You* is actually quite powerful. But in a merely consumer driven fake-emotion context, it inevitably brings disappointment.

[102] Another Radiohead tune, prominently featured in the Leonardo Di Caprio version of *Romeo and Juliet.*

Once she returned from her rounds for a break, I casually asked, "So, what's your favorite movie moment that occurs on an airplane?" She tilted her head to the side and took a moment to ponder. She smiled, and said she couldn't think of anything. The 13–year–old inside of me wanted to mention *Snakes on a Plane*, but my better half knew this would have betrayed my credibility as a conversation partner. Worse, it might have incited a rumor amongst eavesdroppers who weren't familiar with the film. This may have led to a riot, and I would have lost my French crush for good, as I'm sure the guests would demand she check under every seat and in every overhead compartment for cobras. People are pretty paranoid, especially at thirty thousand feet.

When she left to bribe a screaming child with crayons, I recalled a number of memorable scenes that occur on airplanes. Pretty much every James Bond movie has one. There's always the "Don't call me Shirley!" line from *Airplane*. Edward Norton's twisted vision of a plane ripping in two in *Fight Club* came to mind, too. That one may be a tad sadistic. And then I thought of one much better than these.

My favorite airplane-scene occurs in the film *Almost Famous*. The fictional band Stillwater has just exchanged their manager for a fidgety, crack addicted Jimmy Fallon, who insists they trade in their tour bus for a plane, because this will help them get famous. So they do, and they set off on their first cross-continent tour. As they lift off, many of the band's members and entourage are experiencing their first plane ride. What a ride it would turn out to be.

The movie is about a fifteen-year-old journalist named William Miller, who is writing a cover story of the band for *Rolling Stone*. He sits near the back with a couple of groupies. The whole premise is that because he's so young, the band doesn't take him seriously as a journalist, and decide to make friends with him in order to show him how cool it is to be a rock star. Then at the end, he has to figure out whether he should be a good journalist, or a good friend.

Anyways, soon after takeoff in this one scene, the plane hits some serious turbulence. Then, just when things started to even out, the plane starts to freefall. Realizing that they may have only thirty seconds to live, each member decides to spill his deepest secrets to the others. The guitarist admits to sleeping with the lead singer's wife. The lead singer admits to sleeping with the guitarist's girlfriend, who, ironically, is sitting three rows behind them, and is also William's unrequited love interest. The band is all there, spilling their secrets to each other, offering each other an undeserved grace if only because they know death is impending, when all of a sudden, the drummer, who hasn't said two words the whole movie, yells at the top of his lungs from the back of the plane, "I'M GAY!!!"

Then the plane steadies, the pilot rejoices and opens the cockpit door to proclaim that everything will be all right. What follows is the most awkward moment of silence in the history of cinema. It's brilliant, really.

So here I am, chatting away about this scene to my new French-Canadian crush, and she asks, "So what song was playing during the crash?"

"I don't know. I'm not sure if anything was playing," I replied.

"But isn't this the whole point what we were talking about earlier, namely, music's ability to bring people together? And to make important moments feel more meaningful?"

"Well, I think someone starts to sing *Tiny Dancer* by Elton John,"[103] I said. Now, I have always hated Elton John. Well, hate is a strong word. I just can't stand "Crocodile Rock" or "Can You Feel the Love Tonight" or "Candle in the Wind." I know, I know, I'm callous. But *this* song... THIS song is *perfect*. This scene, when these friends join together to sing in innocent chorus at the top of their lungs:

Hold me closer, tiny dancer,

Count the headlights on the highway.

Lay me down in sheets of linen,

you had a busy day today

... this scene is *perfect*.

The perfect scene made so by the perfect song. This is music at its most powerful: joining people together, uniting them not only in harmony, but also in a spirit of forgiveness and grace. In this way, music transcends melody and becomes spiritual. That's why, when John Lennon sang about us "sharing all the world,"[104] we believed him, because

---

[103] This scene actually occurs just a little while previous in the film, after Russell nearly kills himself at a house party. It basically serves the same purpose, however. (I may be stretching the bounds of artistic licence just a tad here.)

[104] In the song *Imagine*

138

music can make us believe the impossible about others, and ourselves, and the world in which we live.

In this film, "Tiny Dancer" gives reference to the band's unity. It serves as a reminder that friendship and life and grace can weather any storm. "Tiny Dancer," with its patient melody building slowly to its joyous climax, is a *perfect* song. And I realized that this scene illustrates perfectly both the reasons that music should be listened to during take-off, and why music should be shared: because it is more powerful than we can imagine.

So screw the rules: we *should* be allowed to underscore the occasional moments of our lives, like taking off in flight, with the right song. Not as mere escape, but because the perfect song reveals that *every moment* is glorious: that *life itself* is glorious. However, life is not an individual event. It is connected, intimately, with the lives of others. Music—*good* music—can help us smooth our differences and find unity when we think it impossible. The patient build of tension and resolution, of the "minor chord and the major lift,"[105] offers a window into the rhythms of grace. And it can teach us, if only we'll let it.

Unfortunately, just before I came to this realization, the turbulence ended, and I was left to share the profundity of my thoughts with my neighbor who responded by snoring in my ear. Cute French-Girl was off serving drinks, I think.

I started thinking about which song could unite most, if not all of the passengers, should the need arise to rejoice with all the frantic sincerity of a group that has just cheated death. The tragedy was, I

---

[105] from Leonard Cohen's song *Hallelujah*.

could only think of two or three songs that most everyone would know the words to. These were "Wonderwall" by Oasis, "Ironic" by Alanis Morissette, and "Thriller" by Michael Jackson. Each less appropriate than the last.

Then I thought of one that might work. It was an old song—a *very* old song. A song that has buried itself into the collective subconscious of the entire English-speaking world, so that pretty much *every single person* on the continent can sing along. It was a song U2 pulled out in their encore last time I saw them, uniting *fifty thousand people* in song—and for a moment, in spirit. It's a song that beautifully illustrates the power that music can wield: that it is more than a product that offers fake fun or fake feeling. Music can reveal the beauty that lies just underneath the surface: it is a voice that can communicate important ideas about who we are, and how our story ends.

And so I whispered softly to myself, in chorus with generations that have gone before me, "Amazing grace, how sweet the sound. That saved a wretch like me. I once was lost, but now, am found. Was blind, but now I see"… with just the faintest hope that Cute French-Girl, or anyone else, just might join in.

Six.

On Technology
Or, *Jesus vs. The Terminator*

Recommended Listening: *Airbag* by Radiohead—because it introduces this chapter in epic sonic fashion, *and* in theme. As Thom Yorke says, "Airbag is... about the idea that whenever you go out on the road you could be killed. Every age has its crazy idiosyncrasies, crazy doublethink. To me, for our era it's cars. I always get told off for being obsessed about it, but every time I get in my car I have to say to myself that I might never get out again. Or I might get out but I won't be able to walk."[106]

Cautionary Warning: In the event you are reading this on a plane, please feel free to read something else, like a vampire novel, or just watch the latest Pixar fare along with everyone else. It's ok, I won't judge.

---

[106] Interview with Q Magazine, Oct '97

Part One: On Airplanes… and Zac Efron

"This is American two-one-three to the cockpit voice recorder. Now we know what it's like. It is worse than we'd ever imagined. They didn't prepare us for this at the death simulator in Denver. Our fear is pure, so totally stripped of distractions and pressures as to be a form of transcendental meditation. In less than three minutes we will touch down, so to speak. They will find our bodies in some smoking field, strewn about in the grisly attitudes of death. I love you, Lance."[107]

1A. "Have a nice flight!" The stewardess smiles at me

with a sincerity that reflects years of practice. She offers a gentle wave, coaxing me towards the on-ramp. A few toddlers sprint past me, quickly reined in and scolded by their mother, who insists I enter first. The whole process feels like a dream, like I can sleepwalk through it in default mode. Stand in line. Show passport. Show ticket. Sit down. Open in-flight magazine. Check movies. Wince at the fact they'll be showing *17 Again…* again. One foot in front of the other. And then I'm in the sky.

Andrew Bird, an indie-darling troubadour I find charming, highlights the pretentious nature of our reliance on technology his song

---

[107] Don DeLillo, *White Noise*, 90

Fiery Crash: "To save all our lives, you've got to envision the fiery crash." It's "Just a nod to mortality, before you get on a plane."

I suppose he's right. There is a healthy fear that should accompany the action of stepping into the bowels of a steel bird—a recognition of the risk I am taking with my life for the sake of modern convenience. The truth is that no one who willingly boards a plane expects it to crash. We have all but forgotten that a fate amongst the "grisly attitudes of death" is a possibility.

Occasionally I'll sit beside someone who grips his armrests a little tighter than I do. When it happens, I feel a strange mix of superiority and pity. *I* fly all the time. *I'm* used to it. I am a fearless creature of modernity. I am Nietzsche's last man.

Today happens to be just such an occasion. I smile smugly at the man: a vain attempt to mask my feelings of superiority. I worry about whether I should engage in some small talk to help put his worries at ease. These types are becoming more rare, but it's interesting to notice the special treatment they still receive. I think the right word is "coddled." The old lady across the aisle offers to hold his hand during takeoff. The stewardess offers a reassuring shoulder touch, and some peanuts, before slowly and carefully explaining that there is nothing to worry about, that planes are statistically safer than automobiles, that it is somehow safer to be thirty thousand feet high than have your feet planted firmly on the ground.

I, however, never really understood the relevance of this argument, because I expect there are much fewer drunk pilots than drunk drivers, and they don't let eager sixteen year olds drive 737's. There's also much less traffic in the sky. So, obviously there won't be as many accidents or casualties. But in fairness to the scared old man next to me, the chances of plummeting to your death surrounded by a group of strangers going haywire are slim to none while sitting in a Toyota. Hence, I'm sure any first time flyers would remain unconvinced by such threadbare reasoning directly lifted from the Flight Attendant Handbook.

I think that being nervous on a plane is healthy. Sitting in a chair while you rocket through the sky is not a natural position for humans. Yet, we have largely forgotten this fact. We have grown accustomed to the various activities we engage in daily that flaunt our victories over the impossible. This is why I agree with Mr. Bird. A little suspicion *is* necessary. Our exploits into the sky do, in a sense, transgress the traditional boundaries of nature, and deserve a moment's hesitation. Because, after a little while, they begin to seem normal to us. But *normal* they aren't. Eating, drinking, sleeping, working: these things are normal. Flying through the sky at a million miles an hour while mowing down cheap microwaveable chicken pasta and watching Zach Effron sing and dance around on a four-inch screen... this is not normal.

2A. I suppose the meaning of "normal" is changing. I

propose that this is a dangerous occurrence. Popping a Xanax and flying to Maui should never be considered "normal." But normal is as normal does, they say. And normal for us includes a pure and utter reliance on technology's many faces, on its subtle but thorough permeation of modern life. Technology's omnipresence coaxes us into a haze of gentle surrender to its awesome power. It has always been there, and it always will be. It provides food, and shelter, and plumbing, and entertainment.

It is a master craftsman at erasing doubt and inspiring submission. It takes care of us.

Consider, for instance, the airport: Technology's Showroom. The environment that saturates the common airport acts like a shot of morphine. There is a reason airports resemble shopping malls, complete with food courts and kiosks. Shopping relaxes us. It is the socially acceptable drug to which we turn for comfort. Even in a plane, if you find yourself getting anxious, you can escape into the world of the "sky mall" and buy some wine from Australia or a watch from Switzerland. If the plane does begin to shake and descend more rapidly than usual, there's always your own personal oxygen mask to comfort you. No, it's not just there to help you breathe. As Tyler Durden[108] explains, "Oxygen gets you high. In a catastrophic emergency, you're taking giant panicked breaths. Suddenly you become euphoric, docile. You accept your fate. It's all right here (in the emergency procedures brochure). Emergency water landing—six hundred miles an hour. Blank faces. Calm as Hindu cows."

Whenever I step on a plane, I offer myself willingly to the gods of technology, those engineers of impossible dreams. Upon their shoulders my very mortality rests. They *have* proven themselves worthy of my devotion. So far. With their help I laugh at traditional notions of possibility. They facilitate an air of arrogance towards the outdated notion that our feet belong planted on the ground, leaving the sky to remain the undisturbed sanctuary of the birds and stars. I can now transcend the bounds of nature, for I am no longer merely human. My life

---

[108] Brad Pitt's viciously memorable character from *Fight Club*

teethes with possibility, with the promise and potential afforded by the mighty tool that Prometheus[109] stole for our benefit: that limitless fire of the gods we call "technology." Armed with this fire, I become like them. Like a god. Free to go anywhere I want, do anything I want. With technology, impossible is nothing.[110]

Technology encourages a certain, shall we say, "elitist" attitude in its users. Armed with technology, we believe we really can do anything: that there is no boundary formed by nature we cannot cross, and no consequence or problem that can't be overcome with... more technology.

What's wrong with this perspective? You might ask. Perhaps nothing. Perhaps everything. All I know is that if I didn't trust technology so... effortlessly... I wouldn't have died in a fiery blaze of twisted metal on the face of a cliff.

3A. Ok, so I didn't actually die in a plane crash. That's a

technique called a "cliff hanger" that, as I learned from its relentless use in *The Hardy Boys* novels, is used to keep the reader interested. BUT ANYWAYS... in October of 2007, I boarded a plane leaving from Katmandu for a small village in the Himalayas called Lukla. I could ei-

---

[109] A character of Greek mythology who stole fire from Zeus to give to humans, and was then punished in the rather macabre fashion of having his liver eaten by an eagle... every morning... after it grew back overnight. The Greeks were nothing if not imaginative. And sadistic.

[110] With technology, or Adidas shoes, apparently.

ther get on this plane, or spend an extra *two months* on my trek towards Mt. Everest Base Camp. Of course, as a loyal minion of modern technology, I chose the quicker, more efficient option.

The runway in Lukla sits intrepidly on a cliff. The small, 18 person craft that caged our helpless bodies dodged over hills and careened towards the side of the mountain before jerking upwards *just in time* to sail over the edge, inches (!) from plunging head on into the rock-face. I disembarked with all the sure-footedness of a jellyfish. I needed ten minutes to catch my breath—to banish from memory the anxieties that were still squeezing my chest—to choose denial.

One year later, almost to the day, I received an email with a link to a news article, and a picture of a fiery assemblage of twisted metal and smoking rubble. The headline read "Plane Crash in Nepal Kills 16 Tourists, 2 Crew." I recognized the runway. And I recognized the plane.

It was *our plane.* I checked the photographs. *The same one.* Yeti Airlines doesn't exactly run a respectable fleet of jets. I suddenly became aware of the risks I'd taken for the sake of fun and adventure. Here was the "fiery crash" of possibility, staring me right—in—the— face. Now, occasionally, I can feel those anxieties return—when I'm on a plane, or driving a car, or using the subway. Sometimes I choose to ignore them. But sometimes, I choose to listen. To let them remind me of the risks I am taking when I place my life in the hands of engineers, pilots, and steel: in men, and their machines. And I sing that song softly to myself... "Just a nod to mortality"... a gesture of respect to the nature of things which I am about to defy.

Part Two: On Airplanes (again)... and Tom Cruise

1B. Did you ever hear that story about Icarus? It's a

Greek myth about a guy whose father fashioned some wings of feather and wax so that they could fly off this island where they'd been exiled. Amazingly, the wings worked. However, Icarus flew too close to the sun, and the wax in his wings began to melt. Since the writers of Greek mythology weren't aware that heat actually *decreases* when you enter the upper atmosphere, and one is more likely to freeze than overheat,[111] this was a believable scenario. So Icarus flew too close to the sun, and his wings melted, and he fell to his death. Big tragedy. He was getting so much pleasure out of this new experience that he became arrogant. He forgot about boundaries and limits and warnings, and went too far. When Icarus lost his fear of nature, he lost touch with the balance that kept him alive.

I'll say that again. *When Icarus lost his fear of nature, he lost touch with the balance that kept him alive.*

Nature is what keeps us alive. Food. Water. Oxygen. Not computers, or iPods, or airplanes. Technology aims to harness the powers of nature, but technology will never fully control or replace nature. We should remember this. We should also remember that nature is still something to be feared, because it is fickle. As well, we need nature more than it needs us. Our relationship with our natural surroundings

---

[111] See *Iron Man*

has always provided a foundation for our human identity. We are connected intimately with nature. It is all around us, and a part of us. In
Genesis, humans were called to be stewards, to look over nature, to cul-
tivate it, but also to respect it. Humans were the beings who were sup-
supposed to take care of nature. We are inextricably linked with nature,
and our religious mindset, our sense of the spiritual, has been woven into this relationship. As *Adbusters* founder Kalle Lasn comments, "When
you cut the flow of nature into people's lives, their spirit dies. It's as
simple as that."[112]

It began when we prayed to the gods for rain, and continued
whenever we needed a mediator to affect nature on our behalf. However, now that we have developed complicated agricultural systems, trade
ships, medicine and other modern conveniences, we don't need to pray
anymore. Now that we can fly around and treat nature like a mistress,
like something to be manipulated for our benefit, we don't need religion. Now that we can exercise considerable control over nature,
religion becomes an afterthought, and traditional notions of humanity—
like being stewards—are lost in a post-modern haze of existentialism
and free choice: a technologically induced trance. When you live in
suburbia, it is easy to forget who you are, and what you were made for.

When we develop this attitude towards nature, like it is something
merely to be used, manipulated for our benefit, I think we run the risk of
'angering the gods,' so to speak. Like Icarus, we are attempting to break
that balance we have relied on for centuries: that healthy fear that keeps
us from falling to our death. Each time I hear about a plane crash, I re-

---

[112] Kalle Lasn, *Culture Jam,* 7

member the story of Icarus. It is all the more tragic because it could have been avoided. However, we have decided that "Business or Pleasure?" for all of us is more important than life or death for some of us.

Perhaps I'm overreacting. But I can't help but consider how quickly my mind would change should I ever find myself in such a situation as a plane crash. I imagine that during the plummet, something like the aforementioned scene painted by Don DeLillo in his book *White Noise* would occur. Brutal honesty is a gut reflex in times of great trauma. The lavish faith we've placed in technology would disappear in an instant. At once, we'd come to despise it, cursing its decadent promises of happiness and control that coerced us so easily, that purchased our loyalty through creative advertising campaigns and carefully selected statistics. A touch of the arm. An offering of peanuts. In a moment like this, we'd inevitably turn back to our roots; back to pleading with invisible deities for salvation, just like our ancestors. We haven't grown out of anything. We haven't evolved, really. We're the same selfish, clueless species, with better clothes and fancier tools. In a hurtling husk of shiny, well–furnished steel, 'superstition' rules the day. Always.

2B. I bring this up to poke holes in two preciously held

beliefs of the modern age. First, that since we have technology, we don't need God. We may not *think* this way, but we certainly support it with our actions. Second, that technology is unquestionably good for us. It took a near death experience (in a sense) to get me to really think about this. You might need one too—though I don't recommend you go looking for one. Anything other than near-death will just drift from memory, and we will retreat back to using the drugs that stimulate comfort and burn away anxiety a la *Brave New World*, the exciting feeling of going somewhere new while sitting in a flying shopping mall that politely demands blind faith.

After my little experience, I decided to sit down and make a list called *Why Planes Are Bad*, just to help my thought process along. Lists are fun.

Ok, so, "Without Planes:"

- We would not be as proficient at war, and thus, at dominating countries in battle who haven't developed an aviation wing of the military.

- We would not have dropped so many bombs.

- We would have avoided 9/11. (The terrorists may have found another way to wreak havoc on us unsuspecting civilians, however, driving a van into a building is much less effective than a plane. Can you imagine? BBSSSHHHGGG! Oh no! The Starbucks! *It's ruined!*[113])

- We would not have witnessed the spectacle that was *Top Gun*, and thus, Tom Cruise's star might have burned out in the '80's, rescuing us from the nightmare of the *M:I* films[114] and *Vanilla Sky*.

- Neither would we have been oppressed by the angst-ridden Michael Bay production *Pearl Harbor*. Or by the actual event at Pearl Harbor, come to think of it. I'm not sure which was worse. Why does

---

[113] Insert random *Scrubs* or *Family Guy*-esque cutaway scene here. My dad doesn't think this joke is funny. But I do.

[114] Ok, the first one wasn't so bad. And the soundtrack by Sigur Ros nearly cancelled out the Cameron Diaz effect to make *Vanilla Sky* watchable. Nearly.

Michael Bay get to keep on making movies? *Pearl Harbor* sucked. And I miss you.[115]

- The TV series *Lost* would've had to come up with another semi-believable premise to get their host of characters onto its mysterious island.

- Ok, once I start referencing *Lost* and *Pearl Harbor,* it's time for my list to stop.

- Oh, I suppose all the people who have ever died in a plane crash would have gone on to live happy, fulfilling lives, before dying of old age. Or the plague.

Thinking critically about something as—let's face it—AWESOME as airplane travel is difficult. Regardless of how many valid reasons I can find to boycott airplanes, we never will. We are addicted to them. They are part of a system that has consumed us, that has given us control and possibilities unfathomable until just recently, and that has also *changed what it means to be human. This* is why we must learn to think critically about such technological advancements as aviation. Our souls, our being, our *destiny* is at stake.

Tyler Durden said that "The things you own end up owning you." Allow me to float a similar thesis: the things you *make* end up *making you.* In a sense, modern technology has made us in its own image: the image of a machine. And what would the image of a machine look like?

---

[115] Shameless *Team America* reference.

Part Three:

Arnold, The God of Technology

4. When I was around six or seven years old, I remember

that the biggest movie around was *Terminator 2*. I saw movie posters in malls and on billboards. I saw the action dolls placed neatly in front of the GI Joes at Toys R Us, and I wanted them. I remember thinking that one day, I'll be old enough to watch this great movie, and understand why Schwarzenegger is such a magnificent hero, and why he comes back, and where he comes back from, and why he left in the first place.

Arnold was pretty much the biggest star in the world at the time, save for Michael Jackson. I remember humbly asking my folks about why we worshipped a guy named Jesus, and not Arnold. "Nobody worships Arnold," Dad replied. This, evidently, was untrue. I remember thinking to myself, "Why isn't Jesus up on billboards? And why doesn't Jesus have his own action figure? Is Arnold better than Jesus?" Maybe he is... after all, I don't think Jesus has laser vision, or a built in rocket launcher.[116] Furthermore, Jesus was killed by a small group of Roman soldiers with, like, swords and whips and hammers. Arnold would have kicked their butts and taken names: ruthless, like a Samson made of steel. The Jews would have loved him. Arnold is much cooler than Jesus, at least in the mind of a six-year-old pop culture junkie.

When Arnold Schwarzenegger gave up the role of *Terminator* villain and became the hero in *Judgment Day*, he went from mere action hero status to that of *legend*. He personified the American ideal—even *with* his accent. This is why he was able to become "the Governator" even though he is thoroughly Austrian: Arnold represents America. Or, at least, everything America aspires to be.

With his huge muscles, Arnold was the portrait of invincibility. He embodied pure intimidation. He fought for justice, and took on all comers. Columbian drug lords, mercenary aliens, kindergarten kids, you name it. To children reared in the 90's, Arnold was the ultimate American role model. In *Terminator 2*, he embodied an ideal of the brains and brawn behind that astutely American orthodoxy that blends heroism and technology into a perfect cocktail of kick-ass awesomeness. In fact, I'm sure that if the spirit of Technology were to incarnate itself, as Jesus was the incarnation of God, it would probably look just like *The Terminator*.

Fifty Percent man. Fifty percent machine.

One hundred percent *awesome.*

I can just imagine the conversation that would take place between these two beings of limitless potential, whose human form

---

[116] Two features found on the toy that were suspiciously absent in the movie.

seriously belies their true essence. If Arnold showed up, everyone would want his autograph. If Jesus also showed, I think nobody would recognize him, and he would probably seem quite unimpressive. A few people might remark that he should hit the gym more often, and perhaps get a fashion consultant.

Nobody wears robes anymore.

"What can you do, little man?" Arnold, the Incarnate God of Technology, might say.

And Jesus might counter with a rebuttal, like, "Well, I can cure the sick! That's impressive, right?"

And Arnold would reply, in his famously strange accent, "Well, I developed a host of machines to treat cancer, to diagnose tumors and bone fractures, and I basically facilitate all of modern medicine which allows billions of people to live healthy and more fulfilling lives. What have you done *lately*, Jesus?"

And everyone would cheer, and whisper to each other that Jesus is lame.

If that didn't put Jesus in his place, the Son of God might brag that he can walk on water. Our audience of modern cynics would be un-impressed by this feat, however, as Criss Angel, that bizarre magician from Las Vegas, has already replicated this "miracle" many times. He has also upped the ante by also walking down the side of a building and through a plate of glass. He can also levitate, and tell you which card you picked. So tricks don't really impress us. We are not as easily conned as those gullible fools who lived in first century Palestine.[117] We need more than a gimmick to win our devotion. We want something tangible, and would thus be more impressed with Technology's offering of a Sea-Doo, which renders walking on water unnecessary, if not simply boring. Why walk when you can ride?

Still, Jesus may argue that he did in fact calm the waters during a storm, a feat yet to be repeated by Mr. Angel, *or* by Technology, though I suspect they are in cahoots. Yet, I'm sure Arnold would reply, "Why would I need to calm a storm, when I've made boats big, strong, and fast enough to go take on any weather system? As well, I can predict when storms may hit, so as to avoid them, should I choose. You just can't beat me Jesus. I am *indestructible*."

More cheers would erupt. Jesus is probably used to this, however, as he dealt with some pretty ornery crowds in his day. They were always asking for signs and miracles, or complaining they were hungry, or shouting that a murderer should be saved instead of him, and that he should be put to death simply because he was unpopular and disappointing, and wouldn't fight the bullies like a good American would. I'm not quite sure why Jesus even bothered, really. If it were me, I'd have taken a page from the book of Cartman: "Screw you guys, I'm going home." And so being booed because he hasn't replicated the wonders of modern technology probably wouldn't faze Jesus.

Just about anything that made Jesus seem extraordinary in his day can be replicated, if not drowned out entirely, by feats of modern

---

[117] Insert actual *Family Guy* cutaway scene here. Yes, they did one about this very subject.

156

technology. Catching tons of fish? Fish farms and larger nets can take care of that. Raising   people from the dead? Please, it's called mouth-to-mouth. And if that doesn't work, use a defibrillator.

How about resurrecting *yourself* from the dead? Unnecessary, as thanks to cloning and stem cell research, pretty soon we'll all be immortal. Just ask Michael Bay, who also directed that sizzling summer hit *The Island,* or Neil Postman, who posited in '98 that just such a scenario—namely, engineering a clone of yourself whose organs can be harvested should you get mangled in devastating scooter accident—is a distinct possibility.[118] And if those don't work, maybe one day we'll transfer our consciousnesses to robots that appear not unlike our hero, the Governator, and live forever as machines.

Hooray!

Perhaps we'll even be ruled by our hero, who took over the state of California, the home of Hollywood, pretty easily. I'm sure if he ran for President, he'd win in a landslide. In fact, how do we know that Arnold S. *isn't* actually a machine produced by Disney's Animatronics team to rule the world?

5. Like The Beatles, technology is "bigger than Jesus." People don't need religion anymore. It's outdated. As the philosopher Martin Heidegger observed, "Technology has become the metaphysic (i.e. religion) of the modern age."[119] It is the de facto faith of those liv-

---

[118] From a lecture at Calvin College in 1998

[119] Craig Gay, *Way of the Modern World,* 81

ing in default mode. Why? Because it makes us feel like gods. Who wants to be a puny human stuck on the ground when we can fly all over the place in our planes and use a Bow-Flex to fashion biceps like Arnold? That's just the beginning. We can now claim almost every quality that once made God unique.

We stand on the edge of omnipresence, as being present in many places at once is easy, thanks to iPhones, Twitter and Google Streetview. We can also achieve omniscience, as no piece of information escapes the authority of Wikipedia—aka, the totality of human consciousness.

Let's see... what are we missing... omnipotence. Right. Ok, well that's an easy one. We can already do just about anything we want. Never in the history of man have we been able to eliminate hunger as efficiently as today, also known as "the age of the microwaveable burrito." Almost no task is outside of the power of technology.

Except for ending poverty. But, whatever. We'll give 'em all cheap cell phones and satellite TV's, so they can watch *Baywatch* and *Seinfeld* reruns too, and everybody will be too amused to notice their problems, just like us. Furthermore, with multi-tasking, I can do it all with my left hand while drinking a grande Verona in the right and steering with my knee.

Oh, what about benevolence? Well, who cares about being good anymore? But even so, with proper social structures that make education, health care and welfare available to everyone, why *shouldn't* we be good? And so, with technology, we *have* become like gods. We don't need salvation from someone else. We trust in the progress of scientific achievement and technological wizardry for *our* salvation, thank you very much.

This is why the notion of dying in a plane crash is so hilarious. At least, to nature it must seem a bit funny. As funny as something as grisly as a plane crash can be. Because what sort of so-called "gods" die in such a manner as this: betrayed by their own creation? As much as we think we are becoming like God, who can control nature at his whim, we can't. We are still humans. Poor, pitiable, depraved, selfish, mortal... *humans*. Still slaves to our fate. Still prone to disaster. Still clueless about the meaning of life and how to achieve happiness. Still the only species that finds it necessary to bitch and moan about a lack of internet at 35,000 feet.[120]

Technology does not save us from disaster. It just changes when and where it happens. Perhaps the frequency occurs less, but can anyone deny that perhaps the greatest disaster of them all—the degradation of our planet's environment—is not caused solely by the economic arms race induced by the Industrial Revolution and the "rise of the machine?"[121] And need I mention the nuclear bomb? You have to admit, it is a lot harder to kill each other with rocks and sticks than with satellite guided nuclear missiles. Technology creates problems, and then sets out to fix the problems it creates. It's a cycle that is spinning out of control.

Call me a conspiracy theorist, but I believe that technology may be planning to solve *all* of the world's problems in one fell swoop. I believe it is concocting a solution that *would* eliminate all possibility of disaster, one that would render earthquakes irrelevant, volcanoes sterile, tsunamis trivial, and global warming completely inconsequential.

[120] see Chapter Two.

[121] Which is, interestingly, the subtitle for *Terminator 3*.

It's simple.

We could leave.

We could take a page from the book of *Wall-E* and leave. Build an ark. Make an ark with our best technologies, fill it with people and fuel and potato chips and maybe some lions[122] and go on a cruise through the galaxy, growing dumb, fat, and complacent as C3PO's cater to our every whim.[123] Surely, this is heaven in the technological age: comfort and excess to the end of our days. We will have been freed from the constricting boundaries of nature forever. Technology will have rescued us from that confining law of gravity, leaving us free to drift wherever we like. Like a rebellious teenager, we'll leave home to discover what else is out there, and forget where we came from, and what made it so special.

However, I can see a potential problem with this so-called "solution."

Because although *we* might leave *nature, nature* won't leave *us.*

Nature is a part of us. That's why they call it human *nature.* There are elements we carry within ourselves that cannot be solved through new technologies. They will never build a device that will cater to the "contours of real human need"[124] without trying to change it. As much control as we may wield over nature *out there,* we will not find the same capacity for control *in here*—in our hearts—unless we start to

---

[122] With treadmills so their muscles don't atrophy.

[123] "Ewww.... I want them to look like Lauren Graham. Make it so." – John G. Stackhouse Jr, my professor at Regent College.

[124] Craig Gay, *Way of the Modern World*, 82

build limits and laws that bind the human heart—that dull the spirited edges of our humanity.

Unfortunately, this is already the direction we are headed. As historian Christopher Dawson commented, "it would be a strange fatality if the great revolution by which Western man has subdued nature to his purposes should end in the loss of his own spiritual freedom."[125]

I can see that this loss is already occurring. I sense it every time I witness a starving child crying on TV and feel no empathy. I realize it when I catch myself thinking about a woman as an object to be used rather than a creature worthy of love. Some would call this "sin"—and it might just be—but it is also how technology is training me to think: how it is shaping me in its image—the image of a machine that is trained to solve every problem in existence, *except* for those that disturb the human heart.

6. I am part of a generation that doesn't care much about history. Through our undying allegiance and everyday use of technology, we have largely forgotten about what it means to join in the tradition of human experience. We have forgotten why wisdom is useful, and why suffering is not to be merely avoided, but sometimes endured for the sake of learning empathy and undergoing spiritual growth. These days, I feel distanced from my ancestors, detached from their ideas and traditions and religions. And I think I know why.

---

[125] Ibid.

It is because "here in my airplane,"[126] I feel superior to them. I know more than they did. I have seen for myself that heaven does not reside just above the clouds. I have reached an aura of enlightenment only available to those who have been above 30,000 feet.

Technology is changing me, and I'm not sure that's a good thing. It makes me wonder where I might be headed, what technology may decide to do with us, with that inherently unpredictable ethos of human nature. After all, we can be quite troublesome, can't we? Fortunately, to quote Stanley Kubrick's *Dr. Strangelove*, "the automated device rules out *HUMAN MEDDLING!*" Perhaps, one day, like in all those Terminator, Matrix and Kubrick movies, the machines will turn on us. They will realize that we are destroying the planet: that we are shameful, selfish creatures, and the universe is better off without us. And just as we became too cool for God, and decided he didn't matter, we will also cease to matter. [127] And the machines will kill us. Either that, or lobotomize the lot of us, and turn the human race into the Borg. Eat your heart out, James Cameron.

The scariest thing about this whole scenario is that in our complacency, we just might let it happen. We already treat other people like machines who perform functions for us. We, in turn, do what we are told. We act like cogs in the machine of capitalist America, never questioning orders, rarely initiating conflict. There was a time when people rebelled; when they led revolutions. When they said "Off with his

---

[126] *Take My Picture* by Filter. My fave song when I was 14.
[127] Which is essentially Nietzsche's criticism of the masses in *Thus Spake Zarathustra*.

head!" instead of, "Our President is an idiot, *but what are you gonna do?*"

There was a time when humans had goals, aspirations, to turn this world into something like the Kingdom of God. Religion was helpful because it reminded us who we are: sinful, childish beings who bicker and fight and are prone to making terrible decisions with our time and money. Religion was there to help us grow into spiritually mature beings, people capable of the compassion and sacrifice that make up real love, so that our goals of peace and prosperity for everyone would become realistic. (In theory). Jesus taught us to look towards the Kingdom of God: to help build Shalom. But today, as Ortega y Gasset comments,

> We live at a time when man believes himself fabulously capable of creation, but he does not know what to create. Lord of all things, he is not lord of himself. He feels lost amid his own abundance. With more means at its disposal, more knowledge, more technique than ever, it turns out that the world today goes the same way as the worst of worlds that have been; it simply drifts.

Like my routine at the airport, we slip into default mode: unaware of our destination, but comfortably lost in the process. If we don't consciously build towards heaven, we will drift towards hell.[128] What else would you call a destroyed planet that can no longer sustain human life?

Without exerting myself to consider the potential consequences, whether they be causing a car crash, ruining the environment, changing what it means to be human or freeing the world from humans altogether—without a "nod to mortality"—we run the risk of fashioning our-ourselves in the image of our new, improved god. We risk forgetting that we were once different: that we could once feel empathy, and compassion, and appreciation, and *love.* That our lives were not always dictated by carefully scheduled day-planners and beeping iPhones, our souls drowning in a sea of information glut.

I think it's a tragedy that I could go a full year without sitting down to watch a sunset, but I can't go a full day without watching television.

Technology is changing me.

It's changing *us.* It is convincing us that the things that make us human, like our relationships with our fathers or wives or best friends, or the select moments in which the beauty of nature captures us, don't really matter. That the times when we feel deep sadness or deep joy, or our when we desire to find a wisdom that can pull it all together in a way that makes sense, don't really matter.

We don't look up at the stars at night, because we're watching our screens glow instead.

We aren't present in everyday situations enough to realize the tender balance of our dealings with other humans, of how our cell phones and computers and TV's begin to become more important than the people around us.

And the more time we spend in distraction, in amusement, the less we spend thinking about what it means to be human; to ask that question that every human should ask himself: *what is it all for?* And as

164

great as these new gadgets are, they really are dangerous, because they disconnect us from others, from being engaged in the moments of everyday life that make up our real reality, and even from ourselves.

The only way for us to find "salvation" with technology is to give up a part of ourselves—a part we might call the "spirit." The part that makes us difficult to control and predict. The part that falls in love without reason. The part that writes symphonies and paints landscapes as an expression of gratefulness. The part that makes mistakes, but finds the strength to overcome them. The part that has ambitions. The part that hopes. In fact, all the parts that make us special: that make life worth living. These don't make sense to the mind of a machine. Yet they are protected by the order, by the balance, between humans and God and nature, which has existed for millennia.

7. There was this Polish film director named Kieślowski who died in '96. You've probably never heard of him, but he was very good. He did a series of ten hour-long films called *The Dekalog*. Each vaguely corresponds to a different selection from the Ten Commandments.

The first features a story about a university professor named Krzysztof and his young son Pavel. Their apartment is filled with computers, and Pavel is infatuated with their ability to solve whatever (mathematical) problem he gives them. The father is a scientist, and a computer engineer. Anyways, it's wintertime in Poland, and Pavel has been given a new pair of skates for Christmas. He wants to try them out on the nearby lake, but his father is concerned that the ice will break.

So over the next few days, the two of them record the temperatures, and do experiments, and basically use their science and computers and technology to predict when it will be safe to skate. Finally, on the night when they have predicted that it will be safe, the professor goes out to try it for himself. He walks out on the ice, and all is well.

The next day, he comes home from work, and Pavel is not there. He is not at his music lessons either, or with his friends. In the distance, Krzysztof notices a crowd gathering at the lake. An ambulance passes him on the street.

He runs over to discover that the worst has happened. Pavel, with confidence in his father's science, had decided to go skating. And the ice broke.

He drowned.

Krzysztof trudges up the stairs to his apartment, listless and frail. He opens the door, and is greeted by the glow of his computer screen. It welcomes him with a message: "I am ready."

But this is a problem the computer cannot solve. It's a problem computers will never be able to solve. Krzysztof, an atheist, makes his way to a church. He enters and falls upon the altar. He violently pushes it over, and begins to weep. A candle falls, and drips wax onto a painting of Mary, just underneath her eyes. It is a beautiful moment. Here, suffering is received, and engaged. Here, a response is offered… and healing doesn't seem so impossible.

⁸ "Now then, listen, you lover of pleasure,

lounging in your security

and saying to yourself,

'I am, and there is none besides me.

I will never be a widow

or suffer the loss of children.'

⁹ Both of these will overtake you

in a moment, on a single day:

loss of children and widowhood.

They will come upon you in full measure,

in spite of your many sorceries

and all your potent spells.

¹⁰ You have trusted in your wickedness

and have said, 'No one sees me.'

Your wisdom and knowledge mislead you

when you say to yourself,

'I am, and there is none besides me.'

¹¹ Disaster will come upon you,

and you will not know how to conjure it away.

A calamity will fall upon you

that you cannot ward off with a ransom;

a catastrophe you cannot foresee

will suddenly come upon you.

- Isaiah 47:8-11

Seven.

On Dreams
Or, *Fight Club at Disneyland*

Recommended Listening: *Where is My Mind* by The Pixies.
For reasons that will soon become obvious.

8:30am. Main Street.

"We are the all singing, all dancing, crap of the world."

As I step through the gates and make my way into the crowd, I am greeting by the smiling, flowery face of a giant cartoon mouse. I approach humbly before the majesty of that familiar visage, a perfect blend of daffodils and magnolias. My euphoria is thick. If my life were a made-for-TV movie, this would be the climax.

I half expect a group of angels to emerge spontaneously and bellow a score to make Handel[129] blush—a suitable soundtrack for a moment I've been anticipating since birth: my first day at Disneyland. It feels like heaven, and home. Like a city built by God himself for the pleasure of his children, and ours.

As I hold my camera at arms length and snap my grinning portrait next to Mickey's, I can feel the vigor rising inside me like Christmas morning. And then suddenly, a disconcerting thought occurs. It penetrates my joy with shame and doubt, like the spiteful words of a jilted lover. Tyler would be so disappointed in me.

I don't have a mentor, but I've always wanted one. Authority figures weren't cool when I was growing up. I learned from films like *Problem Child* and *Home Alone* that being an eight-year-old rebel was cool. We don't need authority figures, because they make rules. They tell you not to blow bubbles in your chocolate milk, not to jump on the couch, and not to watch *Friends* or *South Park*. Still, I grew up casually wishing I had a big brother type of figure to show me stuff like how to throw a football or get a girlfriend. Since I don't have an older brother––or girlfriend—I look for role models in the same place I look for advice on girlfriends: movies. My role models are my favorite movie characters. And like many guys who feel somewhat emasculated by modern society and its spirit crushing restrictions, my favorite movie character is Tyler Durden.

---

[129] Handel is the guy who wrote that 'Hallelujah!' song. Not the one covered by Jeff Buckley. The other one.

Tyler Durden is the foul mouthed, loudly dressed individual played by Brad Pitt in *Fight Club*.[130] This film came out in 1999. That same year, *Office Space, American Beauty*, and *The Matrix* were also released. Coincidence? I think not. This was the penultimate year of a violent century in which humanity learned to "lock up their spirits,"[131] and became slaves to "the machine."[132] Each movie has a protagonist that works in a cubicle and then basically goes nuts. Each is a commentary on the spirit-crushing monotony of the corporate world and our precarious relationship with technology. One man chose to work at McDonalds (for ironic reasons); another to sabotage his office with carefully placed salmon; another to fight wraith-like computer programs. None, however, rebelled with the wicked zeal of Edward Norton and Brad Pitt in *Fight Club*.

Fight Club takes the *Karate Kid* 'protégé/mentor' mold and runs with it. The film is not just about fighting. It's about friendship, mostly. It is a friendship that helps Edward Norton's nameless protagonist learn how to strip away the layered social veneer that has become his identity: to reject the chic lifestyle that has maimed his masculinity and left him spiritually impotent. Tyler teaches his apprentice to purge himself of everything that contributed to his shiny, soulless identity: everything from possessions to hygiene to fashion sense to fear itself. And here, at Disneyland, Tyler's voice is emerging—a manifestation of my troubled

---

[130] A movie based on Churck Palahniuk's book of the same name.

[131] Lyrics from Radiohead's *Subterranean Homesick Alien*

[132] Namely, the Macbook.

subconscious, I suppose—and encouraging a similar purge, puncturing my tapestry of illusion with brisk sound bytes of harsh wisdom.

"You are not a beautiful and unique snowflake."

I can almost sense him next to me, looking over my shoulder at Mickey Mouse's grinning face. I'm twenty-three years old and I'm... conflicted. I stand at a crossroads: caught between selling out my hard earned scraps of hipster credibility and wasting seventy bucks. Unfortunately for Tyler, frugality is a wicked trump card.

I've wanted to visit this place since I was, like, five. I've dreamt about it. This has been my life-goal: to visit this modern day utopia, this earthly attempt at heaven. The place "Where Dreams Come True!" I've come expecting the world, because this is what was promised by countless advertisements and inspiring testimonials.

I've come to *live*. To touch fingers with my childhood heroes. To recapture the imagination and emotion and excitement that once overflowed in my youth. I've come to escape the confining routine of the everyday, and like Peter Pan or Pinocchio, jump headfirst into a land of fantasy. And that anti-consumerist conscience that's been drilled into my psyche by repetitive viewings of this particularly disturbing film won't shut up. *Tyler* won't shut up. He's ruining it for me.

"This is your life, and it's ending, one minute at a time."

If coming to a children's theme park is what I've looked forward to more than any other goal—if *this* is the culminating event in my life, the fulfillment of my dreams—what does that say about me? What kind of life have I lived? My whole life, I rejected dreams I deemed unrealistic: dreams of fighting Nazi's, curing cancer, and changing the world. Clichés. Who needs 'em when you've got Disneyland?

My pride stirs to life in an effort to shield against Tyler's apho-
ristic onslaught. Maybe this dream *is* a bit selfish and hollow, but damn
it, I've worked *hard* in my life, and I *deserve* some excitement. I deserve some freakin' fantasy. This is why I'm here. I mean, *where else*
in the world can you find so many trenchant human desires—to fall in
love, to go on an adventure, to live inside a fairy tale, to live happily ever after—explicitly catered to, each within walking distance of the next?
Disneyland is like a vending machine for the greatest things in life. And
that doubting, sarcastic voice continues to speak the bitter truth:

> *"Life is not a weekend retreat."*

9am. Adventureland.

I check my map and start to plan the day ahead. There are five or
six different sections to the park, but the three biggest ones being Adventureland, Fantasyland, and Tomorrowland. It's still pretty early, so I
think I'll hit Adventureland and the *Indiana Jones* ride first, to avoid the
lines.

As I walk through the winding caverns past spiders, skeletons and
jungle brush, my sadistic shoulder devil dressed in red leather suggests I
set it all on fire, Project-Mayhem-style.[133] A symbolic act of purging
those shameful addictions to Disney-sponsored escapism I've clung to
since childhood.

> *"Only after disaster can we be resurrected."*

---

[133] Project Mayhem is the name Tyler Durden gives to his group of anarchist trouble
makers.

In *Fight Club*, Tyler leads a campaign of destruction in an effort
to realign the perceptions of the general populace. He blends terrorism
and humor into a new art form. As tempting as committing an act of
veritable terrorism in this post 9/11 world would be, I have neither gas,
nor matches; nor an undiscovered penchant for random acts of senseless
violence.

The *Indiana Jones* ride is the park's most popular amongst
tweens and Disneyland veterans. Its appeal doesn't lie solely in the cool
set pieces or clever gimmicks, like the puffs of air that simulate poison-
ous blow darts whizzing past your nose. No, its charm lies in this: for a
moment we are permitted to enter one of our favorite stories. We get to
feel what it's like to be Indiana Jones, a real man's man, who does adventure like Chaplin does slapstick. When we get on the ride, it's kind
of like we're invited into his world, where spiders and snakes and voo-
doo dolls inject a little mystery and danger into our dry, routine, default
life. We are invited to a world where danger is real. This makes every
moment feel acute and exciting.

Unfortunately, the rush only lasts a couple of minutes. As soon
as the ride is finished, the effect wears off very quickly, leaving me
wanting more. So I wait in line to ride it again, and again. However, it
soon becomes predictable, and tiresome. I know what's coming next. I
know the rock won't actually tumble into my car and crush me and my
six-year-old ride mates like roaches. Even though Disney might put up a
convincing illusion of danger, safety rules the day. And though safety
might keep us healthy, it also breeds complacency. The *Indiana Jones*
ride, it occurs to me, is not real adventure. It is a cheap replica of real
adventure, like the *Jungle Cruise* replica of real Africa. When you've
actually been to Africa, you know there is no substitute. At first the ride

is fun and interesting. But soon, it starts to feel campy. After a while, it begins to feel... oppressive... like just another empty promise: just another strange routine.

"How much can you know about yourself, if you've never been in a fight?"

Disney doesn't seem to understand what an adventure *is*. I think a real adventure requires three things:

1)   Goals

2)   Risks

3)   Virtues

Take Harrison Ford's timeless model, for instance. His goal is usually to help rid the world of oppressive forces like the Nazis. He risks his life in pursuit of this goal again and again. He is also good. We wouldn't cheer for him if he were out for mere personal gain. His virtues include not only courage, but also selflessness, humility, and even piety. These virtues, in fact, save him in all three films (most obviously in the last one: "The penitent man will pass!").[134] It's also why we like him so much. If he weren't a good person, we wouldn't care about him. A worthy goal, a risk, and a set of virtues—these are what every main character in a good adventure story needs.

However Adventureland requires none of these of *its* characters: namely, us visitors. Here, you don't need to be good, or try to rid the

---

[134] I realize there is a fourth one, but I prefer to pretend that it never happened, partly because Harrison Ford got old, but mostly because I can't take Shia Labeouf seriously after watching *Even Stevens* that one year we mysteriously got the Disney Channel for free.

world of evil, or take unnecessary risks with your life. And so our adventure feels unconvincing and unsatisfying. Disney tries to compensate for this desire to be part of a good adventure story, and does so better than most. Still, they fail, because an adventure is supposed to be *lived*, not engineered. It is supposed to have real risks, and real rewards, and require something from us. This ride offers a fleeting rush that feels adventuresome, but without any of kind of structure or sacrifice, it ends up feeling hollow.

It leaves me wanting more. I have tasted adventure, and I want *more*. But, as G. K. Chesterton said,

> The perils, rewards, punishments, and fulfillments of an adventure must be real, or the adventure is only a shifting and heartless nightmare. If I bet I must be made to pay, or there is no poetry in betting. If I challenge I must be made to fight, or there is no poetry in challenging.[135]

The same rings true in life. I think we must be reminded that life rests on a precarious balance of moment to moment, that it might end suddenly and without warning, for us to really make the most of our time. When we begin to feel safe and secure, like life is something we are entitled to, something we don't need to work and sacrifice for, we become complacent and stop enjoying it.

This is how I feel a lot of the time. In my life, I have no oppressive enemy. I have no need to risk my life for humanity. I'm sure most people would do just fine without me. I also see no need to be virtuous,

---

[135] Chesterton, *Orthodoxy*

because this is a dog eat dog life—and it's all about the Benjamins, ba-by—and if it feels good, do it—and so on.

Maybe this is why my life feels so boring. Popular culture, like this ride, overwhelms the complexities of life with an entertainment bo-nanza. For a while it feels exciting; but before long, it renders the rest of life innocuous, even tiresome. I have tasted life, but now I want *more*.

10am. Fantasyland.

As I leave behind the *Indiana Jones* 'adventure,' my musings are interrupted as I spot *Splash Mountain* in the distance. Fun fact: this ride is based on the all-but-forgotten Disney film *Song of the South,* which hasn't been re-released on DVD due to content that is overtly racist. Racism is actually pretty commonplace at Disneyland, if you know where to look. But since most of its patrons are giddy children and their stressed out parents, nobody seems to notice.

My inner child takes the reins and directs me towards the steady screams of those brave souls who forgot to bring a poncho and are now soaked. A pair of fat twelve-year olds rushes wildly past me, command-ing their mother to buy them more Churros. On the other side of the street, some too-cool teens line up for the 3'oclock parade of *High*

School Musical 3, their parents nowhere to be seen. A band plays Mary Poppins tunes while standing on the corner. Various costumed characters walk past me, each seemingly ready to burst into song. The mood is other-worldly. Tyler would probably say the cheer is nerve chafing.

"We are all part of the same compost heap."

After waiting twenty-five minutes in line and taking the plunge, I check out my picture on the monitors by the exit. Just as I thought: that unmistakable look of wincing constipation synonymous with pure terror. No, Disney, I will not purchase your overpriced wallet-sized proof of my inner cowardice, *thank you very much!*

I take a tour through *The Haunted House* before strolling over to Fantasyland. Here I find rides inspired by the some of the bulwarks of Disney's illustrious history: Snow White, Pinocchio, and Peter Pan. I think a little about each movie while waiting in the lines, considering how each may have shaped me in some way. I remember that Pinocchio learned that it's best not to tell a lie, and that if you become a hedonist, you might just turn into an ass.[136] I remember that Peter Pan never wanted to grow up, because he knew he would forget how to have adventures and how to fly. I think that really, he didn't want to grow up because he didn't want to lose touch with his imagination, which allowed him to see life as one big adventure. Too late for me, I guess. The wonder that once filled my life with color has since been drained to a pale gray.

Like an adventure story, a fantasy such as Pinocchio or Peter Pan is supposed to teach you something about life. For instance, the les-

---

[136] True dat. (Double True!—shameless SNL/Andy Samberg reference)

son that in life, things like wonder and imagination are important. Or that it is a huge blessing just to be born a "real boy." Whether we are conscious of it or not, stories like these offer us insight into life. As screenwriting expert Robert McKee explains, "story isn't a flight from reality, but a vehicle that carries us on our search for reality, our best effort to make sense out of the anarchy of existence."[137] Stories are vehicles. They take us places in order to show us things that we might not see without their help: like who we humans really are, and how fantastic life itself truly is.

At Disneyland, however, these stories are turned *literally* into vehicles which don't offer wisdom or insight about life, but mere entertainment. They are, truly, "flights from reality." There is nothing real about them. Like *Indiana Jones,* they are too repetitive to be meaningful, and too safe to be convincing. Not that we should loosen a few screws or anything. But after going through a few of these rides, I begin to feel like all the stories I once treasured have been somehow... corrupted. These epic tales of adventure and romance... reduced to two minute thrill rides. Experiences cooked up for quick and easy consumption. Single-serving helpings of joy.

I've found that this tendency to reduce a story into an experience to be bought and consumed isn't present only at Disneyland. It's starting to happen at home, too. This is just how our culture has come to treat stories.

Now, if there's anything absolutely true about humanity, it's that people like stories. Good stories. Fantastic stories. In the past, they

---

[137] Robert McKee, *Story*, 2

helped us make sense of life. They changed our perspectives. They challenged us to feel new emotions, and by telling tales that ran parallel to our own lives, beckoned us to use our imaginations for the betterment of this world.

Storytelling in this day and age, however, has become a lost art. Instead of letting stories inform our lives, they are treated as cures for our boredom. We consume them, and move on to watch another, and another. And if the story is *really* good, we give the director an Oscar, or turn it into a theme park ride at Disneyland, Universal Studios or Six Flags.[138]

More and more movies are coming out which rely on stories that feel more like theme park rides than narratives. Recently the end-of-days movie *2012* came out, which one reviewer described as "eye searing disaster porn." As well, James Cameron's film *Avatar,* the first live action sci-fi 3D film ever, was released, and raised the bar for utterly unrealistic sense-blasting escapism. It quickly became the biggest grossing film of all time and was nominated for nine Oscars.

Many people were interviewed after leaving the colorful 3D world of Pandora and testified to feelings of depression. Their own lives could never match that of what they'd just experienced. Real life could not compare with this shimmering illusion, with this spectacle. I'm sure many people would describe a similar feeling upon leaving Disneyland.

For film, this is a return to its roots, of sorts. Before it became a medium for storytelling, film was simply a spectacle. It was a source of

---

[138] They just opened up a new Harry Potter theme park in Orlando, California. I wouldn't be surprised if, by the time you are reading this, they've made an Avatar ride somewhere.

mere amusement: moving images that carried our minds away from ourselves for a few seconds. Most people are distressed by the image-saturated expectations of modern life, and seek escape into films that won't remind them of their own troubles. Instead of rebelling against the systems that invoke these anxieties, we retreat from these feelings, and pay handsomely to escape to Disneyland or Pandora. Instead of demanding that our filmmakers give us artistic, insightful perspectives on life that inspire us to change things, to change *ourselves*, we've come to prefer the soothing mantras of illusion. And this is what we get: an endless parade of superhero movies, *Shrek* sequels, Judd Apatow comedies and death defying thrill rides. We can now experience adventure, friendship and romance without having to even go outside.

So what happens when we bend a story to our desire for instant gratification, for spectacular escape? What happens when we turn stories into theme park rides? For starters, they become dated very quickly. Our desire for instant gratification is wedded to our desire for things shiny and new. A few years ago, *Lord of the Rings* was all the rage. But since then, it seems we've outgrown it. And I never hear about people reading it anymore. We just watch the movies. By taking a great story and turning it into a ride or a spectacle, we take that story from being timelessly compelling and relegate it to obsolescence. The story loses its ability to speak to our situation from a timeless perspective.

As well, when we read the stories, and tell them to our children, we become a vital part of that story's fabric. We imagine the characters' faces, voices, and clothes. We invest our*selves* in the story, becoming like a character within it. When the only stories we encounter occur on-screen, where they are not told *by* you but *at* you, our imagination is not sparked: it is dulled. Imagination *itself* starts to feel obsolete, because it could never match that of Peter Jackson and his glorious team of special effects wizards.

This is a dangerous occurrence. Some thinkers warn us that this treatment of story forebodes the end of civilized culture, because it deadens the virtues of democracy: namely, the moral responsibility and engagement of its citizens. Instead of crafting stories that will help shape us for generations to come, we turn on the TV and let Disney do it. However, storytelling is a communal responsibility. When we ignore that responsibility, consumer society turns storytelling into a commodity and it stops performing as it's supposed to. As Robert McKee warns,

> When storytelling goes bad, the result is decadence...
> a culture cannot evolve without honest, powerful storytell-
> ing. When society repeatedly experiences glossy, hollowed
> out, pseudo-stories, it degenerates. We need true satires
> and tragedies, dramas and comedies that shine a clean light
> into the dingy corners of the human psyche and society,
> and if not, as Yeats warned, "the center cannot hold."[139]

As I scratch the surface of my discontent with Disney, this is the question I am uncovering. How much longer can we live like this? What will happen to us if we become incapable of dreaming about a better (real) world, and instead, dream about going to Disneyland? What happens when a whole culture dreams of nothing but "wealth, power, fame, plenty of sex and exciting recreational opportunities"?[140]

"The centre cannot hold."

---

[139] Robert McKee, *Story*, 12

[140] Kalle Lasn, *Culture Jam*, 57

The entire world cannot fit into this city. We need better dreams, and better stories to inspire them.

11am. Lunch.

As I sit down with a bread-bowl of clam chowder at Old New Orleans, I reflect on what I've learned so far. A good story, like a good adventure, needs three things. It needs a worthy ambition or goal: the more risky and farfetched the goal, the better the story. It needs its character to risk his life, his fortune, or at least his dignity, to reach that goal.[141] Finally, it needs an ending that depends not upon the character's talent, or strength, or an act of God, but entirely upon his ability to engage his problem and take up his responsibility as the story's protagonist. He must act virtuously. He must "choose wisely."[142] He must have an answer to that question that Tyler is reminding me of every few minutes:

"If you died right now, how would you feel about your life?"

If I had to answer that one, I guess I'd say that I worked, I slept, bought some stuff, and one day, I went to Disneyland.

What a gripping tale *that* is.

I wish I lived a better life: a better story. A good story is a blueprint for a good life. And to live a good life, we must also "choose wisely."

---

[141] For the best example of risking one's dignity, watch Chaplin's *The City Lights*.

[142] From the old (OLD) man in the third Indiana Jones movie.

182

Good stories help this process by drawing us into parallel universes—even ones in galaxies that are far, far away—thereby encouraging us to see the wonder and mystery that live just beneath the surface of our own lives. They warn us against ourselves, and guide us towards better ends. They are able, as movie critic Roy Anker explains,

> to make the familiar distant and strange, briefly yanking viewers out of their accustomed blinkered ways of perceiving the world and themselves. The result is a certain sense of wonder tinged with apprehension, for such moments of strangeness spook people into an acute, if fleeting, awareness of the particularity and finitude of their own mortal lives, the inescapable fact of their fragile aliveness and consciousness.[143]

Good stories help us "behold with wonder the exquisite beauty of ordinary human life."[144] My perspective turns inward, helping me to notice the peculiarities of myself as well as the peculiarities of my world. However, when good stories are co-opted by the good people at Disney and turned into sense-blasting Indiana Jones rides, or dazzling *Avatar* sequels, they lose their ability to help me "choose wisely." When rides and movies become our central medium for the intake of stories, we are rendered complacent and disaffected, like a drug addict after a moderate hit.

---

[143] Roy Anker, *Catching Light,* 345. In a review of *American Beauty.*
[144] Ibid.

I think drug addiction is a good metaphor for most of the Red Bull drinking tweens that walk the streets beside me. "To a drug addict," explains our old friend Chuck Klosterman, "life becomes incredibly simple. There is no history; no rhyme or reason to life; there is no purpose, besides 'get more cocaine.'"[145]

Likewise for most children, there is no purpose besides "get more Disney." Disney is like cocaine for children. Once they outgrow this innocent brand of storytelling, they look for fixes in other media, like *World of Warcraft*, Comedy Central and alt-rock music, which also target and manipulate their instincts to find their life's fulfillment in an easily obtained artificial high. Rock music, adventure movies and fantasy games become like drugs we may partake in a number of times a day to find a spiritual or emotional fix. And after a while, we become dependent on their sweet rush of unreality. We want more, as each rush-inducing medium pledges to give us, as Allan Bloom says, a kind of,

> premature ecstasy… (which) artificially induces
> the exaltation naturally attached to completion of the
> greatest endeavors—victory of a just war, consummat-
> ed love, artistic creation, religious devotion and
> discovery of the truth. Without effort, without talent,
> without virtue, without exercise of the faculties, anyone
> and everyone is accorded equal right to the enjoyment
> of experts. In my experience, students who have had a
> serious fling with drugs—and gotten over it—find it
> difficult to have enthusiasms or great expectations. It is

---

[145] Klosterman, but from *Killing Yourself to Live* this time.

as though the color has been drained out of their lives and they see everything in black and white. The pleasure they experienced in the beginning was so intense that they no longer look forward to the end... They may function perfectly well, but dryly, routinely. Their energy has been sacked and they do not expect their life's activity to produce anything but a living.[146]

The default life of modern existence. Run by experts, devoid of creativity, its vigor bled dry. Brought to you by Disney, the company that lets you experience the best that life has to offer before you hit age seven.

Bloom's words sting, because I can feel their penetrating truth. My life is largely lived in search of instant adventure, romance, excitement and wonder. I have no great expectations or enthusiasms, because I already feel like I've experienced everything life has to offer, or has ever had to offer, or ever will, thanks to IMAX films and video games and theme park rides. Access to these artificial hits of life, each consumed in a safe, virtual environment, quickens the senses but dulls my spirit. They require nothing of me. No courage. No risk, or goal, or virtue. This doesn't make me good, or happy. It renders me docile; complacent; unsatisfied. Deep down I know that life is not supposed to be entirely safe, or easy, or fun. It's supposed to be hard. A little bit dark, and a little bit dangerous. It's supposed to be an adventure.

Don't get me wrong. I don't have a beef with Peter Pan or Pinocchio. If anything, I should thank them for helping me to realize

---

[146] Bloom, *The Closing of the American Mind*

something important about modern life. That these rides, and the rushes I get from them, however trivial, are harmful. They don't help me to live a more fulfilling life when I go back to the real world. In fact, they do the opposite. They make real life harder to live, as I find myself constantly wishing I could escape it and go back to Disneyland: a place where fantasies, though unconvincing, are at least partially realized. Like a potent drug, Disneyland drains the dramatic color from my own life, distills it, and sells it back to me for not only the price of a ticket, but one much steeper: the price of my enthusiasms, and my ambitions. The price of— as cliché as it sounds—my soul.

"We're the middle children of history. No purpose or place. We have no great war, or depression. Our great war is a spiritual war. Our great depression is our lives."

I think I've stumbled upon a great conspiracy.

We are all, most of us, living like drug addicts.

The drugs might not be illegal, but they can be equally as addictive. Comfort. Success. Entertainment. Red Bull. They don't fill my life with color. They drain it. They rob me of the ability to enjoy anything that hasn't been purchased and carefully packaged. I had to visit Disneyland to realize this, but really, I should have just paid closer attention to *Fight Club*. Because really, Tyler thought of it first:

"Do you know what a duvet is?... It's a blanket. Just a blanket. Now why do guys like you and me know what a duvet is? Is this essential to our survival, in the hunter-gatherer sense of the word? No. What are we then?... We're consumers. **We are by-products of a lifestyle ob-**

session. Murder, crime, poverty, these things don't concern me. What concerns me are celebrity magazines, television with 500 channels, some guy's name on my underwear. Rogaine, Viagra, Olestra."

And, of course, Disneyland.

(Now, please turn your cassette tape to side B for part two of Sam's crazy day at Disneyland.)

Eight.

On Endings
Or, *Revolt or Die*

Recommended listening: *Circles* by Thrice
"True progress means,
matching the world to
the vision in our heads.
We always change the vision instead.
We set sail with no fixed star in sight.
We drive by Braille and candle light."

"I end where I began—at the right end.
I have entered at last the gate of all good philosophy.
I have come into my second childhood."

-    Chesterton, *Orthodoxy*

In his book *Four Arguments For the Elimination of Television,* Jerry Mander describes how humans are being uniquely shaped to fit their environment. There is a system in place upheld by technology, permeated with media and driven by the corporation that affects nearly every aspect of our daily lives:

> On the environmental end of the equation, the goal
> is to turn raw materials... into a commodity. On the
> personal end of the equation, the goal is to convert the
> uncharted internal human wilderness into a form that
> desires to accumulate the commodities. The conversion
> process within the human is directed at experience,
> feeling, perception, behavior and desire. These must be
> catalogued, defined, and reshaped... The conversion of
> natural into artificial, inherent in our economic system,
> takes place as much inside human feeling and experi-
> ence as it does in the landscape... **In the end, the
> human, like the environment, is redesigned into a
> form that fits the needs of the commercial format.**[147]
> [148]

Mander is describing an idea that is cropping up all over the place, in films, music, and books like this one. Society is trying to turn

---

[147] Mander, *Four Arguments,* 119

[148] !!!!!!!!!!... Um, ya, so this is like the point of the whole book. Just thought I should point that out.

us into *Sim*-like beings that are programmed to purchase and are incapable of expressing a desire that does not correlate with a system-approved product or experience. So instead of looking for love, we watch a romantic movie. Instead of learning to play an instrument, we buy a CD. And instead of dreaming of changing the world, we dream about going to Disneyland.

Mander describes a laboratory experiment "which mirrored this process of reshaping needs to fit environment."[149] Some chimpanzees were put in a room with twelve buttons, each with a function that provided for a certain need. There was a button for bananas, and one for water, and even one for hugs.

"The chimpanzees' world of experience was reduced to what they could ask for with these buttons. What could be requested, of course, was limited to what the scientists had thought to provide."[150] The scientists conducted the experiment to test the monkeys' intelligence, so I'm guessing the philosophical parallels were probably lost on them. Fortunately, they weren't lost on Mander, who noticed that "confinement itself, the removal of a creature from its natural habitat into a rearranged world where its ordinary techniques for survival and satisfaction are no longer operative, produces several inevitable results:

1) The creature becomes dependent for survival upon whoever controls the new environment. It will use its intelligence to learn whatever new tricks are neces-

---

149 Mander, *Four Arguments*, 119
150 Mander, *Four Arguments*, 119

190

sary to fit that system. If it takes tricks and changes to stay alive, then that's what it takes.

2) The creature becomes focused upon (addicted to) whatever experiences remain available in the new environment.

3) The creature therefore reduces its own mental and physical expectations to fit what can be gotten.

Confined creatures that cannot fit this pattern go crazy, revolt or die."[151]

...

I guess it doesn't matter whether you're a monkey or a human. The choice is simple. Revolt, or die.

I check my watch. Half past three. The shadows are getting longer, and the streets, busier. People are already lining up along sidewalks for the evening parade. I secretly hope that Ariel, *The Little Mermaid*, will make an appearance. I wonder if she'd stay in character if I asked for her number.

"Sorry, we don't have cell phones under the sea. The reception isn't very good."

---

[151] Mander, *Four Arguments*, 119

I trek fearlessly through the castle-themed gates of Fantasyland and straight past the iconic *It's A Small World* ride, where an array of multi-cultural mechanical puppets sing harmonies in perfect English.

I direct myself towards Tomorrowland, and look upon a horizon of spinning rockets—an appropriate metaphor for our fantastic techno-logical age. *"PHENOMENAL COSMIC POWERS!"*, to quote the Genie in *Aladdin*, but nowhere to go: nothing to do but spin in circles.

At this corner of the park, the main attractions include *Space Mountain*, the Toy Story inspired *Buzz Lightyear* ride, the *Innoventions* museum, and *Star Tours*, which feels more like a portal to the '80s than a trip to the forest moon of Endor. But we'll get to that one later. The whole vision of the future here presented feels very retro, with robots, spaceships, and gadgets that already feel outdated. The future, it seems, is stuck somewhere in the past.

There is a monument where you can read a speech from the opening ceremonies of this section of the park. On that day, under the formidable Californian sun, Walt Disney himself proclaimed, "Tomor-row can be a wonderful age. Our scientists today are opening the doors of the Space Age to achievements that will benefit our children and gen-erations to come. The Tomorrowland attractions have been designed to give you an opportunity to participate in adventures that are a living blueprint of our future."

Walt was right on, wasn't he. If Walt envisioned a place where the middle class can get together to play with new gadgets, watch mov-ies in 3D and spend their waking hours in constant amusement, he was spot on. You might even call him a prophet.

Of course, fifty years removed from Walt's speech, we have traversed this future. We have seen what marvels science and technology

can build for us: the iPhone, hybrid cars, 60-inch TV's, genetically indestructible corn. (Still no jet packs though). We live in an age of limitless
information, where humanity's best technologies can fit into the palm of
your hand so you can play Angry Birds while waiting in line. It *is* pretty
great.

Still, humanity's most trenchant problems remain unsolved. We
still have drug addicts, and child soldiers, and racism; not to mention our
old enemies hunger and disease, which still linger mysteriously along-
side the resources and technology needed to alleviate them. Our
blueprint, however, remains the same.

We still wax poetic about a world where scientific achievements
will make life even more comfortable and interesting. We believe in ex-
plorations into space, if only to find new places to plant our flag. We
believe in building a wonderful age where everyone can be amused by
watching Disney movies, even those in the poverty-stricken third world
who live in cardboard boxes and don't have clean drinking water.

We may call our dreams realistic. But really, they're just medio-
cre.

Fifty years ago, Walt's speech probably sounded impressive,
like there was real hope in his vision of things to come. Today, however,
it's obsolete. We have built that future, and called it Disneyland. The
climax of history. A living, breathing, smiling city of fantastic rhetoric
about adventure, imagination and mystery. Push a button, get what you
want. Just like monkeys in a cage.

I came here looking for something. A dream, perhaps. At least, a
reminder of the dreams I used to have. And the realization is slowly
dawning on me that this is not what I've wanted at all. This is merely a
socially acceptable, system-approved route to find satisfaction for my

needs for adventure, mystery, and fantasy. Thrill rides. Makeup. Costumes. A charming illusion.

I cannot be trusted with real adventure, because I'll get hurt. As well, there are few if any real mysteries left, so we try to make them up. And so, I reduce my "own mental and physical expectations to fit what can be gotten." But what can be gotten is no longer good enough. *Disneyland* is not good enough. And since I don't feel like dying, maybe I need to revolt—against this world, against the system, against Disney and the safe and shiny satisfaction it promises. I need to stop being obsessed with living through Disney-certified stories and learn to become the hero of my own story. Although, if Disney is my enemy, does that make me the villain?

In many movies, even Disney ones, the villains are revolutionaries. They want to upset the given order and take control of the tribe. *Mulan, The Lion King,* and *Aladdin* all share the same basic storyline. Someone is threatening to take over the tribe, or the city, or the empire, and therefore, this person must be stopped, because the given order needs protecting. I guess I've been subconsciously programmed by clever animation artists to believe that the natural order of things is good. It is not to be disturbed. But for all we know, Jafar might have actually made a better ruler than Aladdin. After all, it's hard to rule an empire when you're always someplace else on your magic carpet making out with your princess girlfriend.

I hear this logic about the natural order of things reinforced by the rhetoric of evolution. Together, they inspire a very laissez-faire attitude amongst my disaffected peers. Our position could be described this way: "Nature is going to do something someday; nobody knows what, and nobody knows when. We have no reason for acting, and no reason for not acting. If anything happens it is right: if anything is prevented it was wrong."[152]

We are evolving, whether we like it or not, to some end, and there's nothing we can do about it. There's no reason to get upset, or revolt. Just play along. Even Tyler is in on it:

"Let's evolve, let the chips fall where they may."

The trouble is, this is *my* future we are talking about—shouldn't I have a say in what it looks like? Wasn't I part of the generation that Michael Jackson said (at the Superbowl in 1993) would change the world? Merely giving in to the progress of technology and evolution means letting this process unfold randomly, without direction. Our ships may be impressive, but their destination remains the same: "Lost amid (our) own abundance, the world today goes the same way as the worst of worlds that have been; it simply drifts."[153] Just like a cruise ship.

I am unwittingly headed towards a future spent playing golf, watching TV and relaxing on cruise ships surrounded by greasy buffets and Elvis impersonators along with the rest of middle class America.

This is the button-pushing future that consumer society is building for me. But I don't want it. I want something else. I want to steer my own damn ship.

---

[152] Chesterton, *Orthodoxy*

[153] José Ortega y Gasset, *The Revolt of the Masses*.

So maybe I need to start a revolution or something. Not that I really know how. If I've learned anything from the movies, I think I need a gun. Or a sword. I also probably need a megaphone, and some loyal minions who will obey orders. Unfortunately, I have none of these. All I have is a mean spirit of discontent and a manifesto of Tyler Durden's witty aphorisms. Plus my iPhone. Where's a freaking guillotine when you need one?

I can't think of many revolutions that were very successful. In fact, I can't think of very many revolutions at all. I think the French had one, but all I know is that they used guillotines, and it was very bloody. A similar thing happened with the Russians. I think Gandhi was pretty successful in his revolution, but I'm not sure if anybody would notice a non-violent protest at Disneyland.

"Why is that guy lying down in middle of Main Street?"

"Let's just walk around him."

"I guess some people just can't handle Disneyland."

In *Fight Club*, Tyler targets all the credit card companies in his revolution, deciding to blow up their headquarters, thus erasing all records of debt and plunging our delicately balanced economy into anarchy. In his vision, we return to our roots: survival of the fittest. Or rather, survival of the people with the most guns, if *Mad Max* taught us anything. I'm not sure if Tyler's is the revolution for me. Plus, I don't think they sell explosives at the gift shop. Though they *do* have muskets and light sabers...

As clever sounding as it was, Tyler's philosophy wasn't very coherent. If you are dissatisfied with this world, as he was, I think the honorable reaction is to try to change it: to build another world—a better world—rather than try to blow this one to smithereens. This makes for a good adventure, and thus, a good story.

Fight Club starts with Tyler helping Edward to see that everything about the consumer world is fake, and that he should move on with his life and stop caring what people think of him. But then Tyler changes. He gets a vision of anarchy, and goes too far. He stops being a hero, and takes on the role of villain, setting up a typical protégé vs. mentor climax.

"You need to forget about what you know, that's your problem. Forget about what you think you know about life, about friendship, and especially about you and me."

In this moment, Edward sees that Tyler must be stopped. But Tyler can't be stopped. Because—wait— spoiler alert!—

Edward *IS* Tyler. Tyler is just a voice in Edward's head—a personification of his subconscious rebelling against his chosen lackadaisical, vigorless life—just like me. Edward starts by rebelling against his routine, and then against the world in general—but in the end, he finds his greatest challenge when he must revolt against *himself.* That is where the true battle lies. He realizes that he has lost control of his wild masculinity, now unleashed on the world like a flood. It is turning violent, and reckless. Desperate for a grip, Ed can't wrench away control until it's too late, and unwittingly initiates a veritable Armageddon of anarchy. The look on his face is PRICELESS.

I do not want to end up like this. I do not want to lose control of myself. Maybe I should restrain my desire for a violent revolution of destruction, as cool as it might be to see the *It's A Small World* children

melt into a fiery pool of hot plastic.[154] I don't *really* want anarchy, mostly because I find it hard to imagine that professional sports, such as
hockey, would continue to run efficiently in a society without rules. For
as the great G. K. Chesterton says,

> Complete anarchy would not merely make it impos-
> sible to have any discipline or fidelity; it would also
> make it impossible to have any fun. To take an obvious
> instance, it would not be worthwhile to bet if a bet were
> not binding. The dissolution of all contracts would not
> only ruin morality but spoil sport... the stunted and
> twisted shapes of the original instinct of man for adven-
> ture and romance.[155]

So maybe I should replace Tyler with a new role model to help
with my revolution. I probably need someone that exists outside of my
own skull. Unfortunately, I can't think of many role models that weren't
implanted by Saturday morning cartoons or ESPN. Maybe I'll find one
on the History channel. They have a piece on Martin Luther King Jr.
running this month. He is probably a good choice. He led a pretty successful revolution, given the fact that the latest American president is
black—though King ended up dying for it.

I wonder if I'll have to die in my revolution against Disney.
Probably. I bet they have a team of snipers on call, dressed as familiar

---

[154] If you're curious, I'm pretty sure they did this on *Family Guy.*

[155] Chesterton, *Orthodoxy*

Disney characters. You can hide just about anything in a chipmunk cos-
tume.

So anyways, Martin Luther King's big revolutionary cry was "I
have a dream!" He probably wasn't dreaming about going to Disneyland. This place may be the land "where dreams come true!"—but only
as long as you're dreaming about roller coasters and pirates makeup, not
ending child slavery. King's dream was actually of a place called "the
Promised Land." "I've seen the Promised Land," he once said. "I may
not get there with you. But I want you to know tonight, that we, as a
people, will get to the Promised Land."

Like Moses, he held up a vision of this place for people to look
forward to in hope. I wonder if *his* "Promised Land" looked anything
like this one. My whole life, *this* has been "the Promised Land"—the
charming city of fun and adventure which I have been unconsciously
steering towards, and against which I have now resolved to revolt. Probably not.

Disneyland is pretty great, but you'd need to be a (very eccen-
tric) millionaire to actually live here. The rest of us just get to come once
every few years, enough to make us curse the banality of our everyday
lives and desire nothing more than to come back.

If I am going to revolt like King did, I probably need to dream of
a promised land, too. I need some other type of city to want to visit, or
live in: one that is even better than Disneyland: one where everyone is
invited, not just the rich. Also, it'd be nice if it didn't get boring after a
couple days. I think this is a worthy goal for my revolution.

In fashioning this goal, I decide to consult my other favorite author, G. K. Chesterton. He says that after I decide upon an ideal city, it
must not change. It must remain fixed in my mind in order for me to

make real progress towards it. For instance, should I want to make a blue city, I might start by coloring everything blue. Grass, trees, even tigers. If I catch and paint just one tiger blue everyday, I will be making progress. However, if I change my ideal every day from a blue city to a green one or a yellow one, I will make no progress whatsoever, and leave only a few wandering blue tigers about: "specimens of (my) early bad manner."[156]

I must resist the temptation to change my mind about my dream city, because it is easier to change one's ideal than to change the world. A good rebellion needs a good dream:

> This fixed and familiar ideal is necessary to any sort
> of revolution. Man will sometimes act slowly upon
> new ideas; but he will only act swiftly upon old ideas.
> If I am merely to float or fade or evolve, it may be to-
> wards something anarchic; but if I am to riot, it must be
> for something respectable.[157]

Hence, if I am to revolt, I need a dream of a new place, like Martin Luther King. A respectable dream. A dream that, like his, imagines a world where people can live together in peace and harmony. A place where we are not bombarded at every turn with hype and distraction and noise that tries to manipulate us and shape us into purchasing machines rather than human beings.

---

[156] Chesterton, *Orthodoxy*.
[157] Ibid.

A city where I can be myself: where I—and *we*—can be truly human. A city unlike the one I am unconciously supporting as I play the role of a good consumer. For this, I need a worthy vision: preferably one that doesn't change. My ideal city must also be as fun, if not more fun, than Disneyland. It must be a place where beauty and fantasy and adventure can exist in their fullest state without sacrificing *me* in *my* fullest state. It must be very intricately balanced, like a great painting: meaning to say, "It must be composite. It must not (if it is to satisfy our souls) be the mere victory of some one thing swallowing up everything else, love or pride or peace or adventure; it must be a definite picture composed of these elements in their best proportion and relation."[158] However, if my dream city is to be perfectly composed, perhaps it needs an artist much more capable than myself to compose it.

My city must be fixed, and it must be artistically complex, in order to hold all of life's beauty in all of its grandeur. But most of all, it must need me to help build it. This is the point where Disneyland fails the most. It is like a glowing vision of heaven already built, one that eclipses anything we could ever conceive of, dwarfing our own dreams in its shadow. It is discouraging, because I could never hope to build anything this grand in my lifetime. Furthermore, it never changes, because its successive owners try to remain true to Walt's vision.

However, I'm sure if Walt was still around, Disneyland would be much different than it is today. Disneyland probably never fully matched the ideal in Walt's head. He didn't build Disneyland merely for his own amusement: he wanted to share a vision of joy with the world.

---

[158] Chesterton, *Orthodoxy.*

There is something honorable about Walt's vision of a city where the shimmering echoes of heaven can be faintly discerned in the laughter of children. He wanted to build a utopia: a place where heaven meets earth. It was a worthy dream—though maybe a tad overly theatrical.

I'm sure Walt would have been permanently on guard against the powers that have since taken over and turned his park into its present form: a business meant to separate you from your money by any means necessary. He would have been constantly tinkering with different rides, changing this and that, welcoming people to make their own suggestions. In this way, we could have all shared in his dream. So maybe by leading a revolution against Disneyland, I am actually leading a revolution to save it.

My ideal also needs to be protected, preferably by someone who won't die and leave it to his greedy children. It must need me to help build it, and then safeguard it from corruption. It must require my undying dedication, and thus, require an undying, or eternal, revolution. After all, if a white post is to remain white, you must continue to paint it so, or it won't be white for very long.[159]

It seems my ambition is very lofty. My vision must never change. It must be really complex and balanced, holding the full weight of beauty and goodness. And it must somehow need me to build it, so that it will feel meaningful to me. Together, these goals make for a worthy dream. Still, I'm not sure how I could ever expect to build something as great as Disneyland, let alone something *better*. But this is exactly

---

[159] to paraphrase Chesterton, again.

what Martin Luther King dreamed of: a place called "the Promised Land." A place that's *even better* than Disneyland.

Since I want to know more about what MLK was talking about, I use my iPhone to check Wikipedia while I wait in line at Space Mountain. At least these long lines give me time to plot my revolution, which is easier to plan thanks to my electronic sidekick. I already have a checklist made out of what *my* version of the ideal city should be like:

1) Fixed (i.e. not changing all the time)
2) Balanced (intricate)
3) Needs me to build/protect

According to the almighty Wikipedia, "the Promised Land" is what the Israelites called the land of Canaan, or modern day Israel, which God had promised to their forefather Abraham. God led them out of a land where they were slaves who were forced to build giant burial chambers and such. This was pretty much the mother of all revolutions, impressive because they didn't use any swords or guillotines.

Now generally, slaves do not just get up and leave. It seems very unlikely that without divine intervention a tribe of people would just peace-out from an empire that counted on slave labor as its central resource. At least, not without a few swords and guillotines. Slaves, in the real world, do not just get up and go. They need someone else to come and get them. Like a Moses, or a Morpheus, or even a Tyler Durden.

So God gets Moses to come and bring the Israelites out of Egypt. Then he gives them a vision of this place called "the Promised Land" where he (as in, God himself) will rule as their king, and where they will have peace and prosperity. The trouble is, the dream never really comes true. At least, when it does, it doesn't last. So the Jews still believe in a day when God will be their king and bring them peace and prosperity in this land, a day that will last for all eternity. Martin Luther King, then, is telling a story. He isn't telling it as a "flight from reality," but is using story in its intended function: as a source of inspiration, wisdom, and strength. King belives this vision, this story, will bring hope to his oppressed people, because it is older, wiser, and infinitely more powerful than anything he could come up with himself.

"The Promised Land" is later referred to in the Bible as "the New Jerusalem," which is a land, and a city, that is open to everyone, not just the Jews. Kind of like Disneyland, only much, much bigger and better.

Let's see if this city meets our criteria. The dream of this city is fixed, "for it existed before anything else." It is complexly balanced, and "quite literally a picture, for I know who painted it." I also needs us to be a part of it: to "contribute exactly the right amount of your own color."[160] And once it is built, it is up to us to protect it: to stand guard against our natural talent to destroy things, to let our dreams drift and decay. But first, we must steady *within* ourselves an eternal revolution *against* ourselves, against our tendency to give in to lesser satisfactions. Especially in this consumer environment, our ideal is always ready to be swept under the rug of new distractions and pleasures. Vigilance is needed to guard against the unbelief and apathy that threaten to rust closed its gates.

But though the dream of building a city like this seems worthy, I find it very difficult to believe in, because it seems so far-fetched, so un-

---

[160] All, again, from *Orthodoxy,* Chapter Seven: *The Eternal Revolution.*

204

realistic. It seems so fantastic that only a child could believe it with his whole heart—perhaps in the same way that only a child can appreciate Disneyland. This fantastic belief, however, is exactly what is required if I am to lead a revolution in this world, which is now controlled by a system, by an *empire,*[161] that seems so powerful, so all-consuming, that it can't be stopped. Everyone, it seems, is plugged in; loyal to it; dependent on it for survival: "And many of them are so inured, so hopelessly dependent on the system, that they will fight to protect it."[162]

And yet, it is my task to believe in the power of another world. A greater world. A fantastic world. A world rescued from the grip of the almighty empire. A world that only children can truly believe in, for only they have the imagination to conceive it, to believe it possible. However, this seems like an impossible task, because my imagination is anemic. It won't let me believe. I have grown up, and become cynical.

Maybe this is why I really came to Disneyland—to reconnect with my inner child: to ignite the spark of wonder and imagination that burned brightly in my youth, that made it easy to believe in something

---

[161] Can you see where this is going?

[162] To quote Morpheus, my previous Hollywood-derived imaginary role model.

greater. Perhaps I am just another of Disney's legion of grown up disciples who return, year after year, in the hopes of rediscovering the one thing that modern life has stripped them of so relentlessly: their innocence. I came to do battle against my cynicism. I came that I might find hope.

Perhaps my disbelief has nothing to do with the reasonableness of the dream and everything to do with the disappointment I've experienced in every other dream I've ever had. I've been fed so many lines about finding contentment, adventure, and romance in this product or that, that I don't believe fulfillment is truly possible. I have lost hope, and given myself over to unbelief, to resignation that this is the best life can get: riding *Star Tours* with a bunch of pale mid-westerners in fake Jack Sparrow dreadlocks sporting t-shirts with wolves on them.

Star Tours is a very uninspiring take on Lucas's famous trilogy. I suppose that if I'd never seen the films before, this ride wouldn't explain why it was so popular. I would think it was lame, like the rest of Disneyland. But I *have* seen all the *Star Wars* movies. Multiple times, in fact. More importantly, I saw them when I was young, so I loved them, and still do.

I can't remember the first time I watched a *Star Wars* flick, except that it must have been the third one, because I remember liking it because of the Ewoks. I imagined having an Ewok as a friend to help me build forts and attack bad guys with sticks. I also liked it because it had a happy ending. The evil empire was destroyed, and Luke found out that his evil father really did have some good in him. Unfortunately, when you watch the ending of a story before the beginning or middle, the climax loses its potency.

Many critics didn't like *The Return of the Jedi* because they felt it wrapped things up too nicely, and they hated the Ewoks for precisely the same reason I loved them: they were a shameless appeal to children.[163] Plus, most movie critics don't like happy endings, because they are inner cynics like me, and don't believe they can actually happen.

The film the critics did love was *The Empire Strikes Back,* probably its dark and depressing nature better reflected their own depressing, "realistic" sensibilities.

As if realism has anything to do with the *Star Wars* universe.

Or ours.

Really, though, this film is the best because it has the best scene in the whole trilogy—the part where Luke battles Darth Vader, and hears those legendary words that continue to echo through cinematic history: "*I* am your *father!*"[164] When I first saw the film, of course, I already knew this fact, so it was hard for me to imagine the depths of intrigue and confusion that were unleashed on the unsuspecting public at first. "What? I thought his father was dead! Shocker!"

---

[163] *How I Met Your Mother* did a whole episode on this issue in season 7. Check it out.

[164] He doesn't actually say '*Luke,* I am your father" like everyone thinks.

Luke himself was pretty shocked. Vader tries to convince him that his destiny is to join the Dark Side, which is also the more powerful side, and probably the cooler side too. I'm sure Luke was tempted by this. But instead, Luke jumps off of the platform, essentially choosing martyrdom over selling out. He probably never went to high school, where one learns to go with the flow and play the game with the cool kids, like Darth Vader. So Luke falls off the platform to his certain doom—except that in the *Star Wars* world, falling twenty stories into a random space chute/slide is a realistic happening, so Luke lives on.

"In this same scene," as Chuck Klosterman (who else?) comments,

> Darth Vader tells Skywalker he has to make a decision: he can keep fighting a war he will probably lose, or he can compromise his ethics and succeed wildly. Many young adults face a similar decision after college, and those seen as "responsible" inevitably choose the latter path. However, an eight-year-old would never sell out. Little kids will always take the righteous option.[165]

To a little kid, there isn't even a choice. Being righteous is the *only* option. You don't sell out your beliefs, or turn your back on friends and mentors. You do what is right, no matter the consequences. Luke hasn't been bred into listless surrender to life's darker realities by an unforgiving barrage of peer pressure, coercive propaganda and sense-destroying theme park rides. Even in tragedy, he has held a measure of

---

[165] *Sex, Drugs and Cocoa Puffs,*

innocence, and hasn't defaulted to just doing what it takes to survive. He still believes in something greater than himself. This kind of behavior, like the presence of Ewoks and happy endings, is much more plausible to the mind of an eight-year-old than it is to grown ups.

This is because kids believe that life is inherently good, and in order to be a hero, you mustn't compromise your dreams or your beliefs for something as trivial as survival. This is why, to children, revolution is easy. Revolution isn't a war. It's a game.

Luke was able to resist the seduction of the Dark Side not only because he had retained a measure of innocence, but because he was trained for the conflict. If you can remember, Luke spends most of this movie under the tutelage of a muppet curmudgeon named Yoda.[166] Yoda is also a mentor figure, and like Tyler, can wield an aphorism with impressive dexterity: "You must unlearn what you have learned," for instance. Eat your heart out, Socrates.

There is this important moment in his training when Luke has to go into this cavern to fight an enemy that is mysterious to him:

Luke: There's something not right here... I feel cold. Death.
Yoda: That place... is strong with the dark side of the Force. A domain of evil it is. In you must go.

---

[166] Don't even pretend that he's not a Muppet. He's like a thousand-year-old Kermit the Frog. And people try to pretend that this film isn't a kids' movie. Any movie with a muppet clearly is.

Luke: What's in there?

Yoda: Only what you take with you.

Yoda is saying that within Luke is a domain of evil. So in this place, Luke battles a beast of his imagination, a manifestation of Vader. Luke uses his light saber to chop off its head, only to see his own face underneath the mask. This is a very profound moment, because Luke learns that he is not just fighting against an evil force that exists *out there*, but one that exists primarily within himself. He must defeat this evil within himself before he can hope to defeat Darth Vader. He must lead a resistance *in his heart* before leading one in the galaxy.

Further in his training, Yoda teaches Luke about the Force. He says,

Yoda: A Jedi's strength flows from the Force. But beware of the dark side. Anger, fear, aggression; the dark side of the Force are they. Easily they flow, quick to join you in a fight. If once you start down the dark path, forever will it dominate your destiny, consume you it will, as it did Obi-Wan's apprentice.

Luke: Vader... Is the dark side stronger?

Yoda: No, no, no. Quicker, easier, more seductive.

Luke must guard against a quicker, easier, more seductive force, because one day, it could dominate him, and destroy his character. He could "become an agent of evil." He could become the villain—and the destiny of the entire galaxy depends on him not becoming the villain.

This is why the movie is so powerful. Amid the fight scenes and special effects and romance and humor, there is a story that parallels our own. And like every good fairy tale, there is a lesson: each of us may become the hero or the villain. Our destiny is not directed by fate, but by choice. We must be on guard against the quickest, easiest, most seductive choices, because they will destroy us. We might lose control of ourselves. And the entire world—nay, galaxy!—depends on us not selling out.

When the Star Wars franchise was resurrected in 1999, viewers were largely unimpressed. *The Phantom Menace* scored a lackluster 62 percent at RottenTomatoes.com and was bashed by many a fan for its lack of soul and irritating new character Jar Jar Binks. Though the movie succeeded at the box office, it failed in the hearts of fans, for exactly the same reason Disneyland failed my expectations. *Phantom* failed because fans didn't want to see a new Star Wars movie for the first time. They wanted to see the old Star Wars movie for the first time. They wanted to visit that moment when they first encountered this story as a child. They wanted to recapture the wonder, imagination, and innocence that once colored their world.

In a similar manner, I didn't just want to visit Disneyland. I wanted to visit childhood. I wanted to visit a place where the most important things in life are not drowned out by distractions and propaganda: where I have retained a measure of innocence, where I can still *believe*.

Phantom failed because, by 1999, those legions of Star Wars fans had grown up. They had become cynical. They had sacrificed dreams of saving the galaxy for dreams of going on vacations. They had sold out. I don't think their collective anger was really George Lucas's fault. Really, Jar Jar is no different from the Ewoks or Yoda. He is also a shameless appeal to children. Instead of focusing on Lucas, the fans' criticisms should have been directed inward. Perhaps they disliked these new movies because they portrayed a journey that more closely resembled their own. And this was uncomfortable for them, because it subtly betrayed their escapist orthodoxy. It reminded them that in reality, most people live lives that parallel Anakin Skywalker more than Luke. We are disciples of the quick and easy... of the 'cool'... loyal minions of the empire: of the seemingly bright, but inherently dark, side. And like Mr. Vader, our egos have won out over our hearts.

I think people like me who really like watching *Star Wars* and visiting Disneyland are looking for something. When we grow up, we want to experience life infused with the color once available in our youth. But we can't. We're not sure how we ever did. So we push new buttons, asking society to help us find a way to recapture that perspective. But the cheap, manufactured outlets don't fully satisfy. So we move from ride-to-ride, fix-to-fix, and game-to-game in search of that satisfaction, when all along we know *deep down* that what we really need is a second chance. And the only answer that truly satisfies is also the one that is hardest to hear. It is the same one that has echoed through eternity.

"You must be born again."

Jesus also had some wise things to say. He was also trying to get people to think differently: to unlearn what they had learned, to recalibrate their perception of reality. In order to understand *his* kingdom, *his* city, "the Promised Land" that *he* was bringing into reality, people had to think differently. They had to start thinking like children.

This is because when you think like a child, it's easier to play the game of life. Here, you don't get a high score through stuff, or sex, or winning. You win by simply obeying your Father, who will take you on adventures, and teach you how to wonder, and leave just enough room for mystery. Children easily recognize their dependence on their Father, and they trust in him with all their hearts. Because of this, life becomes easy, and satisfying. To them, being righteous isn't difficult—it's just being loyal to the one who made you. It's just being the person you're supposed to be.

Becoming "born again" is like getting a second chance at childhood. It is a chance to kill your old, complacent, *Sim*-like self, and be reborn, so that you may find innocence again. So that you may see the world like a child again. This is the path of rescue laid out for us, and the only effective revolution against the deflating monotony of this default life, because it is first a revolution against yourself. And when the chains fall, the freedom we find isn't a sea of choice—it is seeing clearly the right choice. It is a freedom that opens eyes to see that the world is full of magic, that life is an adventure, and that it is a huge blessing to be born a "real boy." It is a freedom that restores. And once you've found it, you won't return to Disneyland in search of innocence, or your dreams, ever again.

As I wind my way back through Main Street, I overhear that the fireworks are about to start. Unwavering, I tread steadily towards the gates. A few seconds later, the first bang erupts like a gunshot, and I turn to catch the glimmers of yellow, orange, and blue light up the night sky as the crowd laughs and cheers. I notice the glow reflect on the faces looking overhead: upon the faces of daughters holding hands with their mothers, on sons hoisted onto their fathers' shoulders.

For a moment, all is as it should be. A perfect world. A heavenly dream.

And yet, I push past them. For I know that outside these walls, there is more to life than Disneyland. Outside are *real* adventures, and *real* mysteries. There is a world that still needs love; a world that still needs bravery.

And amid the clamor of the crowds, I can hear another voice. A still, soft voice. One that penetrates my shame and doubt, with *joy*, saying, "You will have real obligations, and therefore real adventures, when you get to my Utopia. But the hardest obligation and the steepest adventure is to get there."[167]

---

[167] *Orthodoxy*.

Outro

Wake Up by The Arcade Fire

"Something filled up
My heart with nothing
Someone told me not to cry

But now that I'm older
My heart's colder
And I can see that it's a lie

...

Children don't grow up
Our bodies get bigger but our hearts get torn up
We're just a million little gods causing rainstorms
Turning every good thing to rust

I guess we'll just have to adjust."

(End of Part One)

Afterword

If you have any questions about what you read in this book, or would just like to continue the conversation, go ahead and tweet me @VancvrSam, or leave a comment on my site. Also, if you enjoyed this book, and would prefer I write more books rather than serve you coffee, please tell a friend. Or ten. You can use Twitter, Facebook, or good old mouth to mouth… oh wait, it's *word of* mouth, isn't it. Yeah, try that.

For more resources, or just to keep tabs on when the next episode of The Default Life comes out, please check out my website, TheDefaultLife.com.

Thanks for reading!

Also, thanks to my friends and family for all your support. You know who you are. You're great.

About the Author

Sam McLoughlin is a twenty-something author/blogger/dreamer who lives in Vancouver, BC. In April of this year (2011) he graduated with a Masters in Christian Studies from Regent College. Before that, he spent a few years at the University of Western Ontario studying Philosophy, before taking a year off to see the world. He grew up as the son of YWAM trained missionary parents, who took the family to live in Zambia when he was nine and ten. He likes movies, coffee, and long walks on the beach—but not if it's really hot, or if there's too much seaweed.